Preach for a Year

#8

104 SERMON OUTLINES

*Two complete outlines
for every Sunday of the year*

ROGER CAMPBELL

Preach for a Year #8
by Roger Campbell

Copyright © 2014 by Kregel Publications, a division of Kregel, Inc., 2450 Oak Industrial Dr. NE, Grand Rapids, MI 49505.

Scripture quotations are from the King James Version.

ISBN 978-0-8254-2682-7

Printed in the United States of America
18 / 5 4 3 2

Dedicated to the memory of
Dr. Leon J. Wood

CONTENTS

PREFACE

As I write this eighth and final volume of the Preach for a Year series, I'm struggling to find words to express my appreciation to the many pastors who have taken my simple sermon outlines and made them their own. Your calls, letters, and e-mails of encouragement have gone beyond my expectations. Thank you!

Now I'm faced with the responsibility of making *Preach for a Year #8* both timely and effective. In order to accomplish this, some of these outlines will cry out for a return to better days and proven practices that have brought constant conversions and growth. Others will call for moving forward in faith, expecting the future to be greater than the past even though new methods may require loving adjustments by pastors and people. Some things about effective preaching are unchanging; they are the constants of the Christian ministry. It is the gospel that saves sinners, and that should be our greatest goal. A sermon without the gospel is no sermon at all.

We most love those to whom we preach. Otherwise, according to Paul, we're not really preaching, just making noise (1 Cor. 13). We must live what we preach, because whether doing biblical exposition from the pulpit, walking down a hospital corridor, sharing our faith in an elevator, or ministering to hurting people while standing in line at the post office, we're preaching every day.

INTRODUCTION

Leon J. Wood was the pastor of my youth whose faithful preaching brought me to faith in Christ. Looking back to those early years of his ministry and my life, what impressed me most was his ability to set the scene of a Bible text in order to make it understandable. Not surprisingly, then, the words "setting and scene" have been handwritten in the margins of hundreds of my sermon outlines through the years, and I'm still striving to keep my preaching as relevant to my hearers as his was to me.

Pastor Wood was destined to exercise his gifts in preparing ministers to preach, so he soon left our country congregation to teach in a seminary where fortunate students could learn the importance of instructing without self-destructing, a technique that needs developing by all who may be tempted to impress rather than simply express biblical truth with humility and love for hurting hearers.

Preach for a Year #8 contains no sermon outlines so deep that, in their preaching, ministers will be acclaimed as eloquent orators who hold their audiences spellbound. Rather, in sharing these simple outlines with pastors, I desire to provide them with structured teaching tools for declaring the unchanging gospel in words all their hearers can understand.

The secret of great preaching, it seems to me, is not being polished enough to impress but humble enough for God to bless.

This is the final volume of the Preach for a Year series. The entire set provides busy pastors with 832 of my outlines, which they can improve and preach as they make them their own.

Roger Campbell

Developing Holy Habits for the New Year

Philippians 4:6–8

I. **Introduction**
  A. *We Are Creatures of Habit (You've heard this before and it's true: "The habits you develop, develop you.")*
  B. *Holy Habits That Will Change Your Life*
    1. Habits that will enable you to start each day right
    2. Habits that will enable you to stop worrying
    3. Habits that will cause you to stop being critical
    4. Habits that will make you a blessing to others

II. **Body**
  A. *Read the Bible First (Phil 4:6)*
    1. "Be careful for nothing"
      a. Faith and fear are opposites
      b. Develop habits that build faith and fight fear
    2. The Bible is the source of faith (Rom. 10:17)
      a. Faith grows through exposure to Scripture
      b. Minds saturated with Scripture develop strong faith
    3. Start the day with the Bible and have a better day
      a. Read the Bible before you eat
      b. Read the Bible before you read or watch television
    4. Bible reading turns our thoughts to the gospel
      a. The gospel is about Christ's death and resurrection (1 Cor. 15:3–4)
      b. This is the greatest love story ever told
      c. When we read the Bible we're being equipped to share the gospel
      d. Majoring on the gospel makes missionaries of us all
  B. *Start the Day Thankful (Phil. 4:6–7)*
    1. Stop trembling and start trusting
    2. Expect God to come through for you
    3. Focus on God's blessings and give thanks

        a. Give thanks for things you've been taking for granted

        b. Give thanks that God loves you; that Christ died for you

  C. *Spend the Day Focusing on Positive Things (Phil. 4:8)*

    1. Focus on things that are true, honest, and just

    2. Focus on things that are pure and lovely

    3. Focus on things that are virtuous and praiseworthy

    4. Focus on positive traits in others and you will become a positive person

III. Conclusion

  A. *Invest Your Day Ministering to Others*

  B. *Give Priority to Soul Winning and Reap Great Blessings*

The Power of a Loving Church

1 Corinthians 13

I. **Introduction**
   A. *What Love Is All About*
      1. Paul's masterful description of love and its importance
      2. He explains what love is and what it does
   B. *Preaching Without Love Is Just Noise*
      1. Eloquence is empty without love
      2. Education is ineffective without love
   C. *Sacrifice Is Just Show Without Love*
      1. Giving is a poor investment without love
      2. Sacrifice is a waste of time and treasure without love

II. **Body**
   A. *Love Empowers Pastors to Love Their People*
      1. Not all Christians are loveable
         a. There are no perfect churches
         b. Some Christians are difficult to love
      2. The pastor must rise above his feelings and love the congregation
      3. Through the love of Christ, Paul acted and reacted in love (2 Cor. 5:14–21)
      4. Every pastor is equipped to follow Paul's example
      5. God empowers His servants to love the unlovely
   B. *Love Enables Christians to Love One Another*
      1. Loving Christians put away all differences
         a. We can forgive differences in the church (Phil. 1:9)
         b. We can overcome differences in our homes (Eph. 5:25–33)
      2. There are many reasons for clashes among Christians
      3. It is easier to be part of a faction than to get into the action, but love brings unity
      4. A loving church has a powerful impact on the community (Acts 2:1–5)
         a. Consider the many reasons for congregational conflict in the early church

   b. Still, they put away their differences and launched a revival in Jerusalem

 C. *Love Energizes Christians to Become Soul Winners*

  1. Evangelism is the missing ingredient in most churches today

   a. How does our church measure up in this important area?

   b. What are we doing to fulfill the great commission (Matt. 28:18–20)?

  2. Compare our passion for souls to that of Christ on the cross

   a. His love for a dying thief brought this sinner to heaven (Luke 23:39–43)

   b. Paul's call to evangelism is a love call to us all (2 Tim. 4:5)

III. Conclusion

 A. *What Is the Love Temperature of Our Church?*

 B. *Let's Discover the Power of a Loving Church*

 C. *Let's Demonstrate What Love Can Do*

 D. *Let Love Begin in You and Me*

The Miracle of Marriage

Genesis 1; 2:21–25

I. Introduction
    A. Creation: A Manual of Miracles (Gen. 1:1–3)
1. All was dark until God began His creative work
2. Then light appeared: "Let there be light: and there was light."

    B. A Progression of Miracles Leading to Life
1. The forming of the firmament and dividing of the waters (vv. 7–10)
2. The earth becomes fruitful (vv. 11–13)
3. Light breaks through (vv. 14–19)
4. Fish and animals are created (vv. 20–26)

    C. The Stage Is Now Set for the Greatest Miracle of All

II. Body
    A. Adam and Eve Are Created in the Image of God (v. 27)
1. Details of the creation of Eve
   a. God causes Adam to fall into a deep sleep
   b. The first surgery is performed (Gen. 2:21)
   c. Eve is created from Adam's rib (v. 22)
2. Adam is introduced to his bride
   a. Probably earth's most beautiful woman
   b. Adam experiences love at first sight
3. Adam describes marriage as the closest relationship of life
   a. "Bone of my bones, and flesh of my flesh" (v. 23)
   b. The miracle of marriage is proclaimed (v. 23)

    B. Marriage Is Brought About by Leaving and Cleaving
1. Marriage involves one woman and one man
2. Marriage brings the closest human relationship possible
3. Matthew Henry on the miracle of marriage:
   "Observe that the woman was made of a rib out of the side of Adam; not made out of his head to rule over him, nor out of his feet to be trampled upon by him, but out of his side to be equal with him, under his arm to be protected, and near his heart to be beloved."

C. *The Miracle of Marriage Makes Two People One*
   1. "And they shall be one flesh" (v. 2:24)
      a. Here is the perfect arrangement for family life
      b. Marriage makes a divine dynamic for a loving family
   2. Paul's call for marriage to picture Christ and His church
      a. Wives submitted to their husbands (Eph. 5:22)
      b. Husbands loving their wives as Christ loved the church (Eph. 5:25)

III. **Conclusion**
   A. *Marriage Should Provide a Sound Foundation for Families*
   B. *Loving Families Demonstrate a Touch of Heaven in Their Lives*
   C. *Make Your Marriage a Miracle Starting Today*

Perfect Peace

Isaiah 26:3

I. Introduction
A. *Peace Is the Longing of Every Heart*
B. *The Three Biblical Dimensions of Peace*
1. Peace with God (Rom. 5:1)
    a. This comes immediately upon salvation
    b. "Peace with God" was the title of Billy Graham's first best-selling book
2. The peace of God (Phil. 4:6–8)
    a. The peace of God comes through total surrender to Him
    b. He then becomes the Lord of the surrendered life
3. World peace (Isa. 9:6–7)
    a. This will be delayed until Christ returns to establish His kingdom
    b. Finally, the world will know real peace (Rev. 19–20)

II. Body
A. *The Perfect Source of Peace*
1. Isaiah called God the source of peace
    a. The virgin-born King prophesied to bring peace (Isa. 7:14)
    b. Isaiah describes these wonderful qualities of Christ (Isa. 9:6–7)
2. The psalmist agreed (Ps. 29:11)
3. Paul agreed too (Rom. 15:33)
4. Perfect peace in our lives a picture of what is to come
B. *The Perfect Solution for Peace*
1. "Whose mind is stayed on thee" (focusing on the Lord)
    a. So many things in this troubled world rob us of peace
    b. Turning our eyes on Jesus provides peace in earth's storms
2. "Because he trusteth in thee"

        a. Faith in Christ enables us to overcome the stresses of life

        b. Faith wins and fear loses because faith drives the clouds away

C. *The Perfect Song for the Peaceful: "We Have . . . Salvation" (Isa. 26:1)*

    1. Isaiah looked forward to a better time

        a. He focused on future blessings rather than present trials

        b. He envisioned his people singing of salvation rather than their sorrows

    2. This powerful prophet foresaw a great revival and envisioned singing about it

        a. He refused to be overcome by problems of his time

        b. The theme of his prophecy here is, the best is yet to come

III. Conclusion

A. *C. H. Spurgeon's Questions:*

    1. "Why are we weak when we have divine strength available?"

    2. "Why are we troubled when the Lord's own peace is ours?"

B. *Ezekiel's Question: "How shall we then live?"*

C. *What Will Our Answers Be?*

A Church of One Accord

Acts 2:1

I. **Introduction**
   A. *A United Church Is Powerful*
      1. Consider the impact of the united early church
      2. Three thousand converts (Acts 2:41)
      3. Five thousand converts (Acts 4:4)
   B. *Why Dissension Develops in Churches*
      1. It is easier to be part of a faction than to get into the action
      2. A lack of love brings division and distraction
   C. *Requirements to Achieve Unity and Power*

II. **Body**
   A. *Church Unity Requires Forgiveness*
      1. Consider the reasons that day for divisions among the disciples
         a. Peter's denials of Jesus before the cross (Luke 22:54–62)
         b. Jesus forsaken by all of the disciples (Mark 14:50)
         c. The doubts of Thomas (John 20:25)
      2. How could this divided group of people work together?
         a. They were willing to forgive one another
         b. Jesus had even forgiven those who crucified Him
      3. A forgiving church puts away all differences to serve their Lord
   B. *Church Unity Requires Fellowship*
      1. Consider the fellowship of Pentecost
         a. The disciples were all present
         b. They saw the value of their meeting together
      2. Those who gathered had purpose and priority on their minds
         a. Their calendars were cleared and their clocks set
         b. No excuses kept them from being together
      3. Christians have always needed each other

21

  a. We need one another to achieve Christian
   growth
  b. We need one another to accomplish the work of
   the church
 C. *Church Unity Requires Focus*
  1. These Christians had heard the Great Commission
   (Matt. 28:18–20)
   a. They accepted the responsibility of carrying
    out Christ's command
   b. They saw world evangelism beginning at their
    front door
  2. We have the same responsibilities
   a. How will we respond to this great challenge?
   b. Are we willing to focus on God's call to reach
    the world?

III. Conclusion
 A. *A United Church Requires Some Sacrifice*
 B. *Are We Willing to Pay the Price?*

Public Invitations Today

Revelation 22:17

I. Introduction

   A. *Public Invitations Have Become Unusual*
1. Many churches have abandoned them completely
2. What are the results of this once accepted practice being discontinued?

   B. *The Greatest Invitation in the Bible*
1. See the location of God's final invitation (v. 17)
2. Note its urgency: "And the Spirit and the bride say, Come. And let him that heareth say, Come. And let him that is athirst come. And whosoever will, let him take the water of life freely"

   C. *Consider the Content of These Calls to Commitment*

II. Body

   A. *"Just As I Am"*
1. Here, without doubt, is the most used invitation hymn written
2. It has been called the Christian wedding march because so many have walked down an aisle to meet their Beloved One at an altar
3. Note its simple and biblical call: "without one plea but that Thy blood was shed for me"
4. Here is a rehearsal of the clear invitation of the Savior for sinners to respond to His calls, and millions have done so

   B. *"Only Trust Him"*
1. What better call than this, that all who are by sin oppressed and needing rest can find it in the One who extends mercy to those who trust Him?
2. Is there some reason to abandon these three words that simplify the gospel?
   a. Should they be traded for a more complicated call?
   b. What words would better explain the urgency of making a decision?
3. Is it time to reverse a musical trend and restore simplicity to salvation?

   C. *"I Surrender All"*
1. Who could improve on this call to total commitment to Christ?
2. Here again are three life-changing words that say it all
3. Is there some good reason for ceasing to use this song of surrender?
   a. What better expression could verbalize Christ's call to follow Him?
   b. Does not the Savior deserve our best?
   c. Consider the impact of fully surrendered people on the world
4. What is to be achieved by ignoring this important message?
5. Are we willing to surrender all to the Savior?

III. Conclusion
   A. *Should We Consider a Return to the Tried and True?*
   B. *Could Revival Result from a Decision to Carry Through?*
   C. *The Courage to Change and Renew May Rest with Me or You!*

God's Moving Answer to Meek Moses

Exodus 3:1–12

I. Introduction
   A. *The Call of Moses*
   1. The former key character of Egypt now tending sheep
   2. A voice from a burning bush will change his life
   B. *God Is About to Free His People from Slavery*
   1. Moses learns he is to be their deliverer
   2. He is surprised by the challenge and asks, "Who am I?"

II. Body
   A. *This Is a Common Question*
   1. All who have been given a great responsibility understand the question
      a. Your pastor understands it
      b. Joshua would later feel as Moses did
      c. Paul understood it (2 Cor. 2:16)
   2. Many church leaders and teachers understand it
      a. The challenge of leadership in any church
      b. How can any of us measure up to the tasks at hand?
   B. *Moses Had Special Reasons to Ask This Question*
   1. He had been well known in Egypt and now was a wanted man
   2. He felt unqualified because he lacked eloquence (Exod. 4:10–12)
   3. He had lost his temper while trying to help his people once before
   4. How could he expect to succeed this time?
   C. *This Question Had a Great Answer*
   1. God had anticipated the reluctance of Moses
      a. He knew all about these excuses
      b. The fears of Moses were no surprise to God
   2. God's reply to Moses would replace his fears with faith
   3. God's answer: "Certainly I will be with thee" (Exod. 3:12)

         a. Now everything was changed
         b. Moses will not have to carry out this mission alone
         c. God will be with him every step of the way, and Moses will succeed

    D. *God's Answer to Moses Applies to All He Has Called*
       1. We should all put away our fears to serve God
         a. There are obstacles to all Christian service
         b. God is bigger than our fears and better than our faith
       2. Regardless of the test or task, we can expect success

III. Conclusion
    A. *Let Every Obstacle Be Overcome*
    B. *God's Word to Moses Applies to You and Me*
    C. *Hear It Again: "Certainly I will be with thee"*

Revive Us Again

Psalm 85:6

I. **Introduction**
  A. *Recalling a Nearly Forgotten Word: Revival*
    1. Remembering great revivals of the past
    2. Names that bring revivals to mind
      a. The Great Awakening under Jonathan Edwards
      b. The Wesleyan revival that changed England
      c. George Whitfield's revivals in England and early America
  B. *Local Church Efforts That Ignited Revival Fires*
    1. The days of itinerant evangelists who changed communities
    2. Extended prayer meetings to bring revival
      a. D. L. Moody: "Every great work of God can be traced to a kneeling figure"
      b. Is there a need for a return to such community-changing efforts?

II. **Body**
  A. *The Psalmist's Plea for Revival*
    1. "Wilt thou not revive us again?"
    2. This is a plea that looks back to better days
      a. A revival of the past is on the psalmist's mind
      b. He longs for a repeat of blessings he remembers
    3. This pleading person is tired of the present pitiful condition
    4. He cries out to God for a return of revival
    5. Do we share his passion for an awakening of spiritual life?
  B. *The Psalmist Sees God as the Source of Revival*
    1. He spurns any thought of working up this needed awakening
    2. He knows no tested formula for promoting public piety
      a. He cries out to God on behalf of his nation
      b. C. H. Spurgeon: This psalm is "the prayer of a patriot for his afflicted country"
    3. Do we remember a better time for our nation?

      4. Do we dare to believe that God is able to bless us again?

  C. *The Psalmist Looks Beyond Remorse to Rejoicing*

      1. "Revive us again: that thy people may rejoice in thee"

         a. The goal of this prayer is rejoicing people

         b. This praying patriot believes the best is yet to come

      2. Can we identify with his optimistic faith?

      3. Do we believe God can bless us with revival again?

III. Conclusion

  A. *C. H. Spurgeon on the Results of Revival: "A genuine revival without joy in the Lord is as impossible as spring without flowers, or daydawn without light."*

  B. *Let Us Dare to Pray for and Expect Revival Again*

Night Shift

John 3:1–15

I. **Introduction**
   A. *The Pressing Need of a Religious Man (vv. 1–2)*
      1. Nicodemus, a ruler of the Jews, came to Jesus at night
      2. Here is a seeking religious man who is lost
         a. He is afraid of public opinion so sneaks to the Savior
         b. Miracles by the Master had caught his attention
   B. *A Seeker Who Learns Religion Doesn't Save*
      1. Lessons Nicodemus learned that night
         a. There is only one way of salvation
         b. Eternal life comes through a new birth
      2. Nicodemus will have to shift his opinion about how to be saved

II. **Body**
   A. *Salvation Cannot Be Inherited (vv. 3–4)*
      1. Nicodemus grapples with the thought of new birth
         a. How can a man be born when he is old?
         b. Can a man return to his mother's womb and be born?
      2. Many think eternal life comes through family ties
         a. They have been born into respected families
         b. They have been taught the basics of the Bible
      3. Jesus begins to unravel the mystery
         a. "That which is born of the flesh is flesh"
         b. "That which is born of the Spirit is spirit"
   B. *Salvation Comes Through a New Birth (vv. 5–15)*
      1. This new birth transcends religious opinions
         a. This should not surprise us
         b. Jesus told Nicodemus he shouldn't marvel at it
      2. Religious background has nothing to do with salvation
         a. Nicodemus was a religious man but he was lost
         b. He must shift his confidence from works to grace

C. *Salvation Has Its Roots in God's Eternal Plan*
1. Eternal life has been God's plan from the beginning
   a. The Savior fulfills Old Testament prophecies
   b. The New Testament is in the Old concealed
   c. The Old Testament is in the New revealed
2. Moses and the serpent pictured Jesus on the cross
3. The death and resurrection of Christ picture salvation

III. **Conclusion**
A. *Nicodemus Had to Be Saved by Faith Alone*
B. *A Religious Life Cannot Atone*
C. *Trust Christ Today; Make Him Your Own*

The Simplicity of Salvation

John 3:16

I. **Introduction**
   A. *The Most Familiar Salvation Verse in the Bible*
      1. Words spoken by Jesus to a confused religious man
      2. Nicodemus, a ruler of the Jews, has come seeking salvation
         a. He has been told he must be born again and doesn't understand
         b. Jesus explained the new birth with this promise of eternal life
   B. *We Need to Follow the Example of Christ*
      1. Our task is not to make the simple complicated
      2. We are to make deep truth understandable
   C. *Jesus Helps a Confused Man Understand*

II. **Body**
   A. *Salvation Begins with God's Love*
      1. "For God so loved the world"
         a. See how all-encompassing God's love is!
         b. It begins at the cross and extends to the world
      2. God's love is available to every sinner
         a. This love reaches out to you and me
         b. How will we respond to such love?
      3. This message must flow from our church to the community
   B. *Salvation Rests on the Price Paid by God's Son*
      1. "He gave his only begotten Son"
         a. This is the proof of God's love
         b. Here is love enough to save sinners
      2. Imagine how this great news affected Nicodemus
         a. He was religious but learned his religion couldn't save him
         b. Now he hears the best news of his life: God loves him
         c. What the Law could not do, God's grace accomplished
      3. The cross guarantees salvation to all who respond to God's call

    C. *Salvation Is Attained by Faith Alone*
      1. Those who believe in Him will not perish
      2. Nicodemus knew nothing of this kind of assurance
        a. He was very religious but lost
        b. Now Jesus assures him he can be saved
        c. His salvation will be by faith in Christ
      3. What great relief this must have brought to Nicodemus!
      4. The same salvation is available to every sinner today

III. Conclusion
    A. *Here Is Hope for Every Sinner to Be Saved*
    B. *Here Is a Saving Message for Every Church Member to Deliver*
    C. *What Will We Do with This Message of God's Love?*

A Great Purpose Statement for Life

John 3:30

I. **Introduction**
   A. *The Birth and Ministry of John the Baptist (Luke 1:5–25)*
      1. Zacharias and Elisabeth childless
      2. Gabriel's promise of John's birth and mission
   B. *The Reaction of John's Disciples to Jesus*
      1. Their jealousy over Christ's increasing crowds
      2. John's statement of purpose
         a. He must increase, but I must decrease
         b. This is a great life purpose statement for us all

II. **Body**
   A. *A Statement of Worship*
      1. "He must increase"
         a. Three words that call for full surrender
         b. Three words that declare who deserves first place
      2. Three words that reveal the common contest of life
         a. Life calls for decisions every day
         b. Here is a statement that declares Christ deserves our worship
      3. John declares his purpose in life is to exalt Jesus
      4. What place does the worship of Jesus hold in your life?
   B. *A Statement of Humility*
      1. "I must decrease"
         a. John has no desire for self-exaltation
         b. He's not living for the praise of others
      2. John had qualifications for popularity and praise
         a. He came from a family of faith
         b. His birth was brought about by a miracle
         c. Crowds traveled far to hear him
      3. John had his proper position in perspective: he was to honor Jesus
   C. *A Statement to Challenge Us All*
      1. How does your goal in life compare to that of John?
         a. Does Christ have first place?

        b. Does your dedication to Jesus increase every day?

    2. Where does humility rank in your purpose for living?

        a. How important is the praise of others to you?

        b. Are you continually striving to be recognized as successful?

    3. What do you see as the greatest challenge in life?

    4. What heavenly rewards will be given for your purpose in living?

III. Conclusion

    A. John's Commitment to Christ Cost Him His Life

    B. Does Your Purpose for Living Honor Jesus?

Job's Life-Changing Lesson

Job 42:1–2

I. **Introduction**
   A. *The Man Who Comes to Mind When Trouble Comes*
      1. A man of faith who lost his family, his fortune, and his health
      2. Why we can identify with Job
         a. All face trials in life (John 16:33)
         b. God is bigger than our fears and better than our faith
   B. *Consider the Monumental Trials of Job*
      1. He lost his family and his fortune
      2. His wife turned against him, suggesting that he curse God and die
      3. He lost his health (was covered with boils)
      4. Friends came to visit him and became caustic critics
   C. *Job Finally Learned That Nothing Takes God by Surprise*
      1. "I know that thou canst do every thing"
      2. "No thought can be withholden from thee"

II. **Body**
   A. *Job's Lesson Applies to Our Families*
      1. Imagine Job's sorrow when his children all died
         a. His seven sons and three daughters lost their lives
         b. A storm struck the building where they were feasting
      2. Here's Job's amazing reaction to this tragedy: "The LORD gave, and the LORD hath taken away; blessed be the name of the LORD"
      3. "In all this Job sinned not, nor charged God foolishly" (Job 1:21–22)
      4. Years later he's still confident this didn't take God by surprise and he's rewarded with seven more sons and three beautiful daughters
   B. *Job's Lesson Applies to Our Finances*
      1. Job had been a very wealthy man (Job 1:1–3)

       a. Suddenly his wealth was taken away
       b. Nevertheless he remained faithful
    2. Later, he would confirm that nothing takes God by surprise
    3. This kind of reaction to trouble is called faith and is rewarded
    4. Job would ultimately receive double what he had lost

  C. *Job's Lesson Applies to Our Future*
    1. Job's future was greater than his past (Job 42:10–17)
    2. The Lord blessed Job beyond his imagination

III. Conclusion
  A. *God Knows All About Our Tomorrows*
  B. *We Can Relax in His Love*

The Peacemakers

I. Introduction
  A. *Jesus Said, "Blessed Are the Peacemakers"*
  B. *Who Are These Blessed Ones?*
   1. They are people who make peace in families
   2. They are people who make peace in the church
   3. They are people who make peace in the community
  C. *What Kind of People Are These Peacemakers?*
   1. They are people who are quick to forgive
   2. They are people who demonstrate God's love
   3. They are people who build up rather than tear down
  D. *Where Are These Valuable People?*
  E. *Let's Find Them and Be Blessed*

II. Body
  A. *Peacemakers Are Quick to Forgive*
   1. Where can we find these quick forgivers?
     a. Look for people with unclouded faces
     b. Look for people tender of heart
     c. Look for people who see the best in others
   2. Jesus was quick to forgive
     a. Remember His forgiveness of the woman at the well (John 4)
     b. Remember His forgiveness of His crucifiers (Luke 23:34)
     c. Remember His forgiveness of the thief on the cross (Luke 23:40–43)
   3. Those rejoicing in forgiveness will be peacemakers
  B. *Peacemakers Demonstrate God's Love*
   1. These valuable people resemble their heavenly Father
     a. They sacrifice for the benefit of others
     b. They are quick to reconcile with those who have wronged them
     c. They take a loving look at situations that divide people
   2. Peacemakers focus on redemption rather than wrath
     a. They refuse to make mountains out of molehills

         b. They focus on reconciliation rather than build-
            ing barriers
         c. Their goal is pulling people together, not push-
            ing them apart
    C. *Peacemakers Are Church Builders*
      1. They create an atmosphere of excitement rather
         than despair
      2. Happy harmony exists in their church rather than
         destructive divisions
      3. Their presence helps form a fellowship of love

III. Conclusion
    A. *Peacemakers Live Like Jesus*
    B. *No Wonder They Are Called the Children of God*

Priorities of the Present

Proverbs 27:1

I. **Introduction**
   A. *We All Face the Priority Question Daily*
      1. What is the most important decision you must make today?
      2. Will today's decisions have eternal results?
   B. *The Danger of Putting Off Important Decisions*
      1. The length of life is uncertain, sometimes requiring immediate action
      2. What priorities demand your attention before the day is through?

II. **Body**
   A. *The Priority of Salvation (2 Cor. 6:2)*
      1. Answers to those who plan to be saved someday
         a. "Behold, now is the accepted time"
         b. "Behold, now is the day of salvation"
      2. Salvation should have priority over success
         a. Success in life can be fleeting and deceiving
         b. All earthly gain is temporary
      3. Successful Saul of Tarsus learned this lesson
      4. Wise ones follow his example and make sure of salvation
         a. Have you settled this important question?
         b. How long do you intend to wait to do so?
   B. *The Priority of Seeking Souls*
      1. Jesus was constantly seeking the lost
         a. The woman at the well (John 4)
         b. Zacchaeus up a tree (Luke 19:1–10)
      2. The disciples were called fishers of men (Matt. 4:19)
         a. Their priority in life was to reach people
         b. We are to be imitators of these caring men
      3. Paul was alert to every opportunity for evangelism
         a. The conversion of Lydia at a riverside prayer meeting (Acts 16:14–15)
         b. The salvation of the Philippian jailor (Acts 16:25–34)

       c. Stand Paul before kings and he will seek their salvation
    4. How important is seeking souls for each of us?
  C. *The Priority of Sending Soul Winners*
    1. Here is the priority of having a part in the Great Commission (Matt. 28:18–20)
    2. Great churches not only go with the gospel but send missionaries
    3. Missionary giving and sending are vital to a healthy church

III. Conclusion
  A. *How Precious Are These Priorities to Our Congregation?*
  B. *Let Us Reclaim These Important Areas for the Glory of God*

Resources for Rough Times

I. Introduction
   A. Fear Is a Monster That Stalks Us All
      1. This enemy appeared immediately after the fall
      2. Fear robs us of adventure and success, making cowards of us all
   B. When Faith Wins, Fear Loses
      1. God gave great promises to Isaiah for overcoming fear
      2. These resources for rough times are available to you and me

II. Body
   A. The Resource of God's Presence
      1. "Fear thou not; for I am with thee"
         a. A Christian is never alone
         b. We can rest on this promise during rough times
      2. "Be not dismayed; for I am thy God"
         a. Storms may threaten, but God is in control
         b. His resources are greater than our problems
      3. Acting on these promises drives our fears away
      4. When faith wins fear loses
   B. The Resource of God's Strength (v. 10)
      1. "I will strengthen thee"
      2. The Lord invites us to trade our weakness for His strength
         a. This transaction empowers us for any crisis
         b. No problem is too great for our Lord to overcome
      3. Hear God's promises in your weakest hour
         a. "I will help thee"
         b. "I will uphold thee with the right hand of my righteousness"
      4. It is always right to trust God no matter the circumstances
      5. On the darkest day, God makes a way
   C. The Resource of God's Promises (v. 13)
      1. "I . . . will hold thy right hand"

    2. "Fear not; I will help thee"
    3. God always keeps His promises
       a. Consider His promise to send a Savior (Luke 1:26–37)
       b. Consider the promise of Jesus preparing places for His own (John 14:1–2)
       c. Consider the promises of the resurrection of Christ and His return (John 14:3–6)

III. Conclusion
   A. Are You Going Through a Rough Time?
   B. Rest on God's Promises and Ride Out the Storm
   C. For Those Who Trust the Savior, the Best Is Yet to Come

Dodging Defilement

Series in Daniel Begins   *Daniel 1:8*

I. Introduction
  A. *The Story of a Prisoner in Iraq (Daniel 1:1–8)*
    1. Daniel and his friends taken captive by Nebuchadnezzar
    2. A testing time for these young men of faith
    3. We all face testing times in life
  B. *Where to Draw the Line*
    1. Daniel decided to be faithful
    2. He chose purity of life rather than compromise
    3. Pleasing God became the purpose of his life

II. Body
  A. *Daniel's Decision Called for Courage*
    1. Nebuchadnezzar held the power of life or death over Daniel
      a. What the king called design, Daniel called defilement
      b. The king planned to control every detail of Daniel's life
      c. Refusing to comply with this plan could result in death
    2. Daniel's devotion was to a higher King
      a. He made a life-changing decision
      b. His decision involved full surrender to his Lord
    3. Who is the Lord of your life?
  B. *Daniel's Decision Called for Full Commitment*
    1. This decision determined his destiny
      a. He would be known as a man of one purpose
      b. His purpose would be to serve the Lord rather than the king
    2. In Daniel's mind, this meant a refusal to defile himself
      a. He had determined what defilement meant to him
      b. Defilement to Daniel meant taking part in the king's diet and drink

43

   3. This young prisoner had decided to dodge
      defilement
C. *What Are You Facing That Could Defile You?*
   1. Is it something that would defile your mind?
   2. Is it something that could identify you with evil
      people?
   3. Is it something that would destroy your testimony
      for Christ?
   4. What steps will you take to dodge defilement?
      a. Will you increase your time spent reading the
         Bible?
      b. Will you make a new commitment to holy
         living?
      c. Will you pray with greater faith?

III. **Conclusion**
   A. *How Will Our Church Be Affected by Your Faith
      Decision?*
   B. *Others Are Watching to See the Outcome of This
      Matter*
   C. *Dodge Defilement by Drawing Closer to Christ Today*

Daniel's Divine Diet

Series in Daniel   *Daniel 1:8–21*

I. Introduction
  A. *Four Prisoners of a Controlling King*
    1. Nebuchadnezzar had plans for these four young men
    2. They would be developed into the king's dream team
    3. This reigning king made the rules they must follow
  B. *Daniel Refused to Follow the King's Diet*
    1. He saw following this diet as self-defilement
    2. Daniel's decision placed him and his friends in danger
    3. This led to a test to see which diet was best

II. Body
  A. *The Characters Affecting Daniel's Commitment (vv. 6–10)*
    1. The king's servant
      a. He was the diet director
      b. He had orders from the king
      c. He risked his life to enable his prisoners to be true
    2. Nebuchadnezzar and his dream diet
      a. The king had goals in mind for Daniel and his friends
      b. He envisioned them being fat and flourishing
    3. Daniel's partners, who joined him in committing to be clean
  B. *The Commitment That Called for a Contest*
    1. Daniel's faith enabled him to issue a challenge
      a. He was confident God would come through
      b. He and his friends must simply be true
    2. There are many challenges for God's people
      a. We must believe God will be up to the occasion
      b. The three young men laid their lives on the line
    3. We must learn to look past the challenge to victory
    4. What is the greatest challenge facing you?
  C. *Commitment to God Is a Two-Way Street*

    1. Daniel was committed to God and God was committed to Daniel
    2. Rejecting the king's defilement diet stood the blessing test
       a. Ten days later the undefiled ones were healthy and blessed
       b. Even the king and his advisors were impressed
    3. These four became very important to the king
       a. They became his trusted advisors
       b. Serving God makes us a blessing to others

III. Conclusion
    A. *God Should Always Have First Place in Our Lives*
    B. *Are We Fully Committed to Him Today?*
    C. *Surrender to Him Without Delay*

Daniel and the Dangerous Dreamer

Series in Daniel   *Daniel 2:1–23*

I. **Introduction**
  A. *Daniel Moved from One Crisis to Another*
    1. Sometimes our lives also seem to follow this pattern
    2. What crisis are you facing today?
  B. *Daniel's Promotion Now Placed Him in Peril*
    1. He had been blessed for standing firm on his convictions
    2. This had brought him into favor with the king and promoted him
    3. Now his promotion placed him in a life-or-death situation
  C. *Keys to Confidence in a Crisis*
    1. Nothing takes God by surprise
    2. No problem is too difficult for God to solve

II. **Body**
  A. *The King's Forgotten Dream (2:1–13)*
    1. Nebuchadnezzar's nightmare roused him from sleep
      a. He was troubled by this dream but didn't know why
      b. He called his advisors to ask the details of his dream
    2. The king's advisors were unable to satisfy the king
      a. They complained that no king made such demands (vv. 10–11)
      b. The angry king called for their execution
      c. Daniel was now facing death
  B. *Daniel's Response to the Crisis (vv. 16–18)*
    1. He declared that God would provide what the king wanted
    2. He then called a prayer meeting with his three friends
      a. How would we respond to a life-or-death situation?
      b. Would we panic or join others in prayer?

47

      3. Daniel and his friends cried out for wisdom in this crisis
        a. We can claim God's wisdom and power too
        b. Personal and church problems can be solved by prayer (John 16:24)

  C. On the Darkest Day, God Makes a Way (vv. 19–23)
    1. God answered the prayers of Daniel and his friends
      a. The answer came that very night
      b. God revealed the content of the king's dream
    2. Lives were spared because God answered prayer
      a. Daniel rejoiced and spread the good news
      b. He and his friends would live and expand their witness
      c. Even the unbelieving other advisors would be spared
    3. Daniel's prayer meeting became a praise meeting (vv. 20–23)

III. Conclusion
  A. People Who Trust God Find That He Is Enough
  B. Let Us Pray in Faith and Expect God to Answer

The God Who Reveals Secrets

Series in Daniel   *Daniel 2:19–49*

I. **Introduction**
   A. Nebuchadnezzar—The Confused King
     1. His forgotten dream had frustrated him to the point
       of murder
     2. The lives of his advisors were in jeopardy
     3. God revealed the dream and its meaning to Daniel
   B. Daniel Brought the Good News to the King
     1. "There is a God in heaven that revealeth secrets"
     2. We must seize opportunities to tell others about our
       Lord
       a. Power and position should not shut our mouths
       b. We're commanded to share God's good news
         continually

II. **Body**
   A. Prophecy Provides an Opportunity for Witnessing
     (vv. 28–29)
     1. The king wanted to know about the future
       a. Many share his curiosity about what lies ahead
       b. Daniel had the king's attention and drove his
         message home
     2. Nebuchadnezzar's eyes were opened to God's pro-
       phetic plan
       a. Daniel was fulfilling his responsibility to God
         and the king
       b. How long has it been since you dared to be like
         Daniel?
     3. Great rewards await those who care enough to share
       this good news
   B. Humility Adds Effectiveness to Witnessing (v. 30)
     1. Daniel gave all the glory for his wisdom to God
       a. He claimed no special intelligence of his own
       b. He pointed out this interpretation was to benefit
         others
     2. Wise Daniel even explained this to help the king
       understand

    a. God was at work in this dream and its interpretation
    b. The whole world would be changed by understanding it
   3. Future students of prophecy would be amazed at its accuracy
  C. *Courageous Witnessing Brings Rewards (vv. 31–49)*
   1. Imagine the courage of Daniel in relating the king's dream
    a. Would the king believe Daniel knew what he was talking about?
    b. Might the king feel Daniel was faking to save his life?
   2. Daniel dared to envision and interpret the meaning of the great image
    a. He saw this as a prophecy involving nations through history
    b. The king believed Daniel and gave him great rewards
   3. Daniel proved it pays to trust God and serve Him

III. Conclusion
  A. *Faithful Witnessing for God Worked Wonders*
  B. *Daniel and His Friends Received High Positions in Babylon*
   1. Rewards await all faithful servants of the Lord
   2. Let's eagerly seize every opportunity to serve Him

The Fourth Man in the Fire

I. Introduction
  A. *Nebuchadnezzar's Desire for Worship*
    1. Pride placed the king in a dangerous position
    2. Solomon's warning about pride (Prov.16:18)
      a. Pride goes before a fall
      b. The king had a fall in his future
  B. *Nebuchadnezzar's Great Golden Image*
    1. He demanded that everyone fall down and worship it
    2. To refuse meant to be cast into a furnace

II. Body
  A. *Three Men Who Wouldn't Bend to the King*
    1. The king's command was clear
      a. Those who refused to bend their knees to the image would die
      b. Standing up for their convictions signaled suicide
    2. Shadrach, Meshach, and Abed-nego stood tall at his call
      a. They saw bending their convictions as grieving God
      b. Paul would later warn against this (Eph. 4:30)
    3. Most believe Daniel was away on some official mission
    4. How would we have reacted to this dangerous decision?
  B. *Three Men Who Wouldn't Bow to the Image (vv. 8–18)*
    1. Enemies of these unbending ones told the king
      a. These Chaldeans had once been his advisors
      b. Now the demoted ones saw a chance to get even
    2. Those who stand tall may be hated by all
    3. Bending would have meant betraying their Lord
      a. These three loyal ones were willing to risk all
      b. They would serve the king but never worship him

    C. *Three Men Who Couldn't Be Burned (vv. 19–30)*
      1. Nebuchadnezzar notices another man in the fire
        a. "Did not we cast three men bound into the midst of the fire?"
        b. The fire only burned off the ropes that bound them
      2. These three men of faith were not alone in the fire
        a. The king concluded one like the Son of God was in the fire too
        b. Those who walk with God are never alone (Matt. 28:18–20)
        c. They are always accompanied by the Fourth Man in the fire

III. Conclusion
    A. *God Rewards Those Who Are Faithful to Him*
    B. *Are You Facing Some Fiery Trial Today?*
    C. *Your Lord Will Always Be True*
    D. *Expect Him to Come Through*

Wanted: Men On Fire

I. Introduction
  A. *Daniel—A Book of Prophecy and Powerful People*
    1. An outline of the ages
       a. Views of the end time
       b. The cross and destruction of Jerusalem
       c. The Antichrist, the tribulation, and end-time rulers
    2. Also a book about people
       a. Shadrach, Meshach, and Abed-nego
       b. The trials, suffering, and triumphs of these men of faith
  B. *Three Men Who Were Tried by Fire*
    1. The command to bow to Nebuchadnezzar's image or burn
    2. They refused to bow but did not burn

II. Body
  A. *These Men Were Different (v. 12)*
    1. They weren't afraid of the king or his golden image
    2. Jesus was different too
       a. He was righteous in a sinful world
       b. He was the light of a dark world
       c. He demanded a different life from His followers
    3. We are to be different because of what Jesus did and said
  B. *These Men Were Daring (v. 16)*
    1. They didn't fear the king
    2. "We are not careful to answer thee"
    3. The thrill of becoming a Christian: a new life
       a. Taking risks for the sake of Christ
       b. Daring to live differently for the Lord's sake
       c. Embracing the challenges of living for Christ
    4. Have we lost the adventure of salvation?
    5. Has the fire of fresh faith departed?
  C. *These Men Were Dedicated (vv. 17–18)*
    1. They declared God was able to deliver them

53

    2. They backed up their faith with true commitment
    3. They were like Job: "Though he slay me, yet will I trust in Him" (Job 13:15)
    4. They were like Jesus in Gethsemane

III. Conclusion
    A. These Fiery Men Were Delivered
        1. Jesus walked with them in the fire
        2. Only their ropes were burned, setting them free
        3. Even the smell of fire was taken from them
    B. God Is Searching for People on Fire
    C. Will We Be Like These Fiery Three?

Weighed and Wanting

Series in Daniel   *Daniel 5*

I. **Introduction**
   A. *A Favorite Text of D. L. Moody*
      1. Moody wrote a book titled *Weighed and Wanting*
      2. His goal was to show how far short Belshazzar fell from God's standard
   B. *The Setting and the Scene*
      1. Israel was in captivity in Babylon
      2. Belshazzar, the king of Babylon, was celebrating his victories
      3. Mighty Babylon was about to be judged

II. **Body**
   A. *The Night of Triumph Became a Night of Terror (vv. 1–6)*
      1. Belshazzar and his friends were having a drinking party
         a. They didn't know that mighty Babylon would fall that night
         b. Soon their coming fall would be written on the wall
      2. Sacrilege would be part of this wicked party
         a. Alcohol often contributes to the fall of people and nations
         b. This night they would drink from sacred vessels dedicated to God
      3. Who would have imagined that judgment was near for these partying princes?
         a. They felt safe but we are never safe in sin
         b. "The wages of sin is death" (Rom. 6:23)
         c. The party was about over . . . judgment was on the way
   B. *The Strange Handwriting on the Wall (vv. 5–9)*
      1. The party stopper: fingers of a man's hand wrote on the wall
      2. The king was so frightened his knees knocked together
         a. His mind was filled with fear and dismay

      b. His advisors had no answer for this strange development

   3. The wise men of the kingdom had no answer for this development

      a. Finally the queen offered a solution

      b. She advised the king to call for Daniel, the dissolver of doubts

   4. This man of God would give advice to the troubled king

  C. *Wise Words for a Worrying, Wayward King (vv. 25–30)*

   1. He was told he had been weighed by God and found wanting

   2. The handwriting on the wall said it all

      a. The sins of the king had caught up with him

      b. His kingdom would fall and his life would end

   3. A lesson for us all: we cannot sin and win

III. Conclusion

  A. *Daniel Was Promoted Because of His Wise Counsel*

   1. This wise prophet was made the third ruler in the kingdom

   2. Wealth and power were given to God's spokesman of the hour

  B. *Sin Has Placed God's Handwriting on the Wall Again*

  C. *How Will We React to God's Call to Repentance and Faith?*

Daniel's Faith Under Fire

I. Introduction

    A. *Daniel Rose from a Prisoner to President*

        1. Daniel and friends had been captives in Babylon

            a. They had rejected the king's food and wine (Dan. 1:8)

            b. Daniel had interpreted Nebuchadnezzar's dreams (Dan. 2, 4)

        2. Daniel had correctly predicted Belshazzar's death (Dan. 5)

        3. Darias, the Mede, appointed Daniel president (Dan. 6)

        4. Kings and kingdoms fall, but God's servants continue

    B. *Darias Saw That Daniel Was Different (Dan. 6:3)*

        1. The king sensed an excellent spirit in Daniel

        2. As a result, Daniel was made top man in the kingdom

    C. *What Can We Learn from Daniel's Life?*

II. Body

    A. *People of Faith May Be Persecuted (v. 4)*

        1. Daniel was despised by others of his time

        2. Serving God has always been costly

            a. Prophets were often jailed or stoned

            b. John the Baptist was jailed and beheaded

            c. All of the apostles except John were martyred

        3. Jesus warned his disciples of coming rejection by the world

    B. *Those Who Live for God Must Expect Problems*

        1. Daniel's enemies searched for faults in him

            a. They were unable to find these hoped-for faults

            b. What a credit this was to this faithful man!

            c. Pilate would later say of Jesus. "I find no fault in this man."

        2. The decree that sent Daniel to the lions' den

            a. Petitions were to be made only to the king for thirty days

        b. Daniel kept praying, petitioning God for his needs

        c. Daniel's dedication sent him to the lions' den

    3. While others were plotting, Daniel kept praying

  C. *Faith Finds All the Help It Needs in Prayer*

    1. Daniel's prayer life was unchanged in spite of his predicament

    2. Even the king had confidence in Daniel's prayers

    3. He believed God would deliver Daniel

    4. God protected Daniel from the hungry lions

        a. God "millennialized" the lions for a night

        b. The king spent the night fasting, and so did the lions

III. Conclusion

  A. *God Protects His Own from Destruction*

  B. *When Faith Proves True Others Are Brought to God*

  C. *Will We Follow Daniel's Example Under Pressure?*

Daniel Saw It All

Series in Daniel   *Daniel 9:1–19*

I. Introduction
A. *Daniel Digs Deeper Than Ever Before (vv. 1–2)*
   1. He gives himself to prayer and prophecy
   2. Books and study become his friends
B. *God Will Reveal Many Secrets to Him*
   1. He learns the importance of confession of sin
   2. Discovering God's will and plan are now his passion
C. *Daniel States His New Purpose in Life (vv. 3–4a): "I set my face unto the Lord God, to seek by prayer and supplications, with fasting, and sackcloth, and ashes: And I prayed unto the LORD my God, and made my confession."*

II. Body
A. *Daniel Gets Serious About Sin (vv. 7–16)*
   1. He sees how sin has brought confusion to his people
   2. He confesses his sins and the sins of his people
   3. He states the cost of sin to Israel
      a. Daniel sees the dispersion of his people because of their sins
      b. Even the kings and princes have reaped the consequences of their sinfulness
      c. He cries out to God for forgiveness and blessings
B. *Daniel Prays for God's Blessings to Return (vv. 17–19)*
   1. He prays for God's wrath to be turned away
   2. He longs for God to hear the prayers of His people
   3. He cries out for answered prayer and for light to replace darkness
      a. He asks for God to listen to the pleas of His people
      b. He pleads for mercy for Jerusalem and its citizens
   4. He reminds God that these people and their city belong to Him

59

        a. Daniel's heart is moved by the needs of his people

        b. He longs for revival that will change their lives

  C. *What Would Daniel's Example Do for Us?*

    1. Would it bring a new awareness of our sins?

    2. Would our church be revived by facing our shortcomings?

    3. Would our community be awakened by seeing a new dedication among us?

        a. Who will make the first move toward spiritual renewal in our church?

        b. Are we as concerned about our church as Daniel was about his people?

III. Conclusion

  A. *God Is Looking for People Who Will Dare to Be Daniels*

  B. *Who Among Us Will Respond to Daniel's Call?*

  C. *Who Will Stop Holding Back and Surrender All?*

    1. Let this day be a time of new beginning

    2. Why should we wait? It's time to respond to God's call!

Daniel's Insights from an Angel

Series in Daniel Ends   *Daniel 9:20–27*

I. Introduction
   A. *Daniel's Prayer for Jerusalem (vv. 16–18)*
      1. This patriot becomes passionate in prayer
      2. He fears the wrath of God may fall on Jerusalem
   B. *Daniel Longs for God's Blessings to Arrive on Time*
      1. He prays for God's face to shine on the sanctuary
      2. He pleads with God to consider their condition and deliver them

II. Body
   A. *Picture Daniel Pleading and Praying for Deliverance*
      1. He longs for God to respond to his prayers
      2. Confession of sin brings forgiveness and blessings (v. 20)
         a. Are we as moved as Daniel in praying for God's intervention?
         b. What awaits our faith-filled praying for our community and nation?
      3. Desperation often precedes deliverance
         a. How desperate are we for God to deliver our nation?
         b. The plan of God would soon be made clear to all
   B. *The Arrival of an Angel to Reveal God's Plan (vv. 20–23)*
      1. Gabriel's arrival was right on time
         a. His words must have greatly encouraged Daniel
         b. The survival of Daniel's people was as sure as the promises of God
      2. Gabriel announces his purpose in coming to Daniel
         a. He has arrived because Daniel is greatly loved by the Lord
         b. He has brought a message about Daniel's future
         c. Daniel will receive skill and understanding
      3. On the darkest day, God makes a way
   C. *God's Timetable Revealed by Gabriel (vv. 24–27)*
      1. The mystery of the seventy weeks

a. Seventy weeks means seventy sevens of years
b. This then means 490 years to introduce the messianic age
2. Daniel was then given a preview of God's great plan of redemption
  a. There would be difficult days ahead but glorious ones too
  b. Christ would come and be crucified to pay for our sins
  c. Our Lord would make reconciliation for iniquity
3. Mysteries about the future remain but some day all will be plain

III. **Conclusion**
  A. *We Must Seize the Time Ahead to Serve the Lord*
    1. Christ will come to resurrect the Christian dead
    2. All believers will be caught up to be with Christ at the rapture
    3. Kingdom living awaits all believers during the millennium
  B. *The Future of Christians Is as Bright as the Promises of God*

Needed: A Truce in the Worship Wars

Ephesians 5:19–20

I. **Introduction**
   A. *What's the Primary Cause of Dissension in Churches?*
      1. Changes in styles of worship have divided us
      2. This is especially true concerning choices and volume of music
   B. *Previous Patterns of Worship Were Predictable*
      1. Singing hymns, Bible reading, prayer by the pastor and congregation
      2. An offering, a sermon; often followed by a public invitation for salvation
      3. Then the worship style revolution arrived, changing almost everything
         a. Great hymns of the faith began to be spurned in favor of praise choruses
         b. Divisions arose according to age, requiring separate services
         c. Young and old people forgot how much they needed each other

II. **Body**
   A. *Have Churches Gone Through Such Changes Before?*
      1. Yes, and often with anger over changes of any kind
         a. Once congregations worshipped by singing psalms
         b. Moves to change this pattern met strong opposition
      2. When gospel songs were introduced, they were thought to be shallow
         a. Congregations considered them too fast for worship
         b. Now they are remembered as great Christian music of the past
   B. *Paul's Call on Music in the Church (v. 19)*
      1. He stressed the need of great variety (psalms, hymns, and spiritual songs)
      2. Paul wrote that Christians should make melody in their hearts to the Lord

   a. Is this true in our congregation?
   b. Do we have blended services with no age barriers?
  3. Love opens the door for true worship
   a. Love makes worship and musical styles acceptable
   b. Loving worshippers can enjoy a broader range of lyrics, beat, and style
   c. Christian love bridges the gaps between personal opinions
 C. *Revived People Would Call a Truce in the Worship Wars*
  1. The music recommended in the Bible would cause us to sing, united in love
  2. John Wesley's advice for singing in the church: "Sing lustily and of a good courage. Beware of singing as if you are half-dead or half-asleep, but lift up your voice with strength."
  3. C. H. Spurgeon's ideal of congregational singing in his church would end most of the worship wars in churches today. The parameters of music in his church were as follows: "No chorus is too loud, no orchestra too large, no psalm too lofty for praising the Lord of Hosts."

III. Conclusion
 A. *We Need a Truce in the Worship Wars That Brings Peace*
 B. *Harmony in Worship Should Be Our Goal*

Good Friday's Earthquake

Matthew 27:27–54

I. **Introduction**
   A. *The Lord's Painful Path to the Cross*
      1. Christ before spineless Pilate
         a. Pilate's wife urged him to have nothing to do with Jesus
         b. Unwilling to do right, Pilate collapsed under pressure
      2. The soldiers mistreated Jesus and placed a crown of thorns on His head
         a. Jesus is taken away to be crucified
         b. Fulfilled prophecy at the crucifixion (Isa. 53:5–6)
   B. *Divine Darkness Descends over the Earth*
      1. The seven last words of Christ
      2. The forsaken Savior pays the price of our sins
      3. Nature responds to this hour of the ages
         a. Darkness descends over the earth
         b. Christ's last cry from the cross

II. **Body**
   A. *How the Earth Reacted to the Death of Christ (v. 51)*
      1. The veil of the temple was torn in two
         a. The way was open now for all sinners to be forgiven
         b. An earthquake shook the entire area
         c. Rocks were broken up by the death of the Rock of Ages
      2. Graves were opened and Old Testament saints were resurrected
      3. This was the hour of the ages prophesied centuries before it happened
   B. *How Has the Death of Christ Affected Your Life?*
      1. Has this gift of God's love moved your heart to surrender to Him?
      2. Has Calvary's earthquake shaken you from your sins?

       3. Are you now ready to commit your life to the One who died for you?

       4. How will you respond to God's great gift of His love?

  C. *See How the Men in Charge Responded to These Miracles (v. 54)*

       1. They were moved and convinced by the earthquake

       2. The shaking earth made them afraid

       3. Their words were, "Truly this was the Son of God"

       4. Are you convinced of this unshakeable truth?

III. Conclusion

  A. *This Is the Time to Surrender Your Life to Christ*

       1. Don't delay another day

       2. Peace awaits your act of faith in the Savior

  B. *Respond to His Love and Be Sure of Salvation*

  C. *Let Good Friday's Earthquake Bring Peace to Your Heart*

An Earthquake on Easter Morning

Matthew 28:1–10

I. **Introduction**
   A. *Two Marys on Their Way to a Grave (v. 1)*
      1. Two grieving women decide to visit the sepulcher
      2. Their faith was small, but a great surprise awaited them
   B. *Easter's Earthquake Changed Everything (v. 2)*
      1. The angel of the Lord descended from heaven
      2. The stone at the grave was rolled away
      3. Victory over death was made official
      4. God still moves the stones that challenge our faith

II. **Body**
   A. *The Conquest of Fear (vv. 3–6)*
      1. The guards of the tomb were afraid of the angel
         a. They had good reasons to be afraid
         b. They were on the wrong side of God's plan
      2. The women were temporarily afraid
         a. Fears are normal under some conditions
         b. Faith would drive their fears away
      3. The resurrection of Christ dispelled their fears
         a. Faith and fear are opposites
         b. Faith drives all fears away
   B. *The Commissioning of Those Who Believed (vv. 7–8)*
      1. "Go quickly, and tell his disciples"
         a. The disciples must hear this good news
         b. Death had been conquered; Christ was alive!
      2. The women accepted their commission and obeyed
         a. Great things were ahead and the good news must be shared
         b. These faithful women were obedient messengers
      3. Why would anyone hold back from delivering this message?
         a. This sacred story still needs to be told
         b. Christ has risen and we must declare the good news

    C. Those Who Obey Meet Jesus on Their Way (vv. 9–10)
1. Once on the move, the women met the Master
   a. Meeting Jesus moved their hearts to worship Him
   b. They heard His voice and fell at His feet
2. Christ's comforting words must be shared with others
3. Great things were ahead and they were part of His plan

III. Conclusion

    A. The Great Commission Would Be Given (vv. 18–20)
1. All power in heaven and earth would be invested in this plan
2. Worldwide missionary work would be placed in their hands

    B. This Would Bring the Greatest "Earthquake" Known to Man

What Time Is It?

Acts 1:1–14

I. Introduction
   A. *The Urgency of This Hour*
      1. God's plan is always on schedule
      2. God's timing has been right through the ages
   B. *The Question That Demanded an Answer*
      1. "Lord! Wilt thou at this time restore the kingdom to Israel?"
      2. Parallels between that time and today
      3. What was the answer to that question of the hour?

II. Body
   A. *It Was Time to Wait upon the Lord (vv. 4–8)*
      1. They were waiting for the promise of the Father
         a. That promise was the coming of the Holy Spirit
         b. We are to wait for the coming of the Son
      2. Their waiting was to be a time of prayer
         a. We know this because of what they did
         b. It was time to pray because of the coming earthquake
      3. It is surely time to pray today
         a. The threatening world situation
         b. Christians—a tiny minority compared to the world population
      4. Without prayer the church cannot survive
   B. *It Was Time to Witness for the Lord*
      1. "Ye shall be witnesses unto Me"
      2. There was a job to do, a world to reach
      3. Most churches are falling short in witnessing
      4. They were to wait and then witness
      5. The difference between their situation and ours
         a. God's next great event for them would empower their witnessing (Holy Spirit power)
         b. God's next great event for us will end our witnessing (the rapture)
   C. *It Was Time to Be of One Accord (v. 14)*
      1. "They continued with one accord in prayer"
      2. The times were too serious to delay witnessing

    3. Deterrents to divisions
        a. Their experience with Christ was fresh
        b. The promise of the Father was about to be fulfilled
        c. The task at hand was urgent

III. Conclusion
    A. The Early Church Met the Challenge Given to Them
    B. Will We Meet the Challenge God Has Given to Us?
    C. Will We Turn Our World Upside Down for Jesus?

New Beginnings

2 Corinthians 5:17–20

I. **Introduction**
   A. *The Christian Life Has a Beginning*
      1. No one is born a Christian; all are born sinners (Ps. 51:5; Rom. 3:10–23)
      2. All need to be born again (John 3:1–5, 16)
   B. *Sometimes Even Those Born Again Need New Beginnings*
      1. When they become bitter about the past
      2. When they are burdened about the present
      3. When they are bothered about the future
      4. David understood this and prayed for a new beginning (Ps. 51)
   C. *Three Dimensions to a New Beginning*

II. **Body**
   A. *Let the Past Be Past Through Forgiveness*
      1. "Old things are passed away"
         a. Let's believe this concerning our past sins (Ps. 103:12)
         b. Let's believe this regarding sins after salvation (1 John 1:9)
      2. Refuse to be tormented by sins God has forgiven
      3. New beginnings also require forgiving others (Eph. 4:30–32)
         a. Many are held back by refusing to forgive
         b. It is time to put away old grudges
      4. We can forgive because we have been forgiven
   B. *Let the Future Be Fantastic Through Faith (v. 18)*
      1. "All things are of God"
      2. We begin with God by faith at salvation (Rom. 5:1; Eph. 2:8–9)
      3. The entire Christian life is an adventure in faith
         a. "The just shall live by faith" (Rom. 1:17)
         b. Faith is total trust in the Lord about everything; the opposite of fear
         c. As faith increases, fear decreases
      4. Why are so many Christians in bondage to fear?

71

   a. They aren't trusting God for everyday
    provisions
   b. They have forgotten that all things are possible
    with God (Luke 1:37)
  C. *Let the Present Be Exciting Through Evangelism*
    (vv. 18–20)
   1. "And hath given to us the ministry of
    reconciliation"
   2. We have been commissioned to tell others of
    Christ's love
    a. We are ambassadors for Christ
    b. We are to bring others to be reconciled to God
   3. Nothing is as exciting as witnessing and bringing
    others to Christ

III. Conclusion
  A. *Have You Begun Your Life with Christ?*
  B. *Have You Lost the Joy of Your Salvation?*
  C. *Forgiveness, Faith, and Evangelism Can Bring a New*
    Beginning

Blessings or Blight

Psalm 1

I. **Introduction**
   A. *A Psalm of Contrasts*
      1. The description of a godly man (v. 1)
      2. What the godly man rejects
         a. The counsel of the ungodly
         b. The path of sinners
         c. The seat of the scornful
   B. *What Makes the Godly Person Rejoice? (v. 2)*
      1. He delights in the law of the Lord
         a. His delight is this continually
         b. He meditates on God's law day and night
      2. He is therefore a positive, praying person
   C. *The Godly Person Is Like a Thriving Tree*
      1. A tree planted by a flowing river
      2. A tree that brings forth fruit continually

II. **Body**
   A. *The Ungodly Are Different (v. 4)*
      1. They are unlike the godly
      2. They are like the chaff which the wind drives away
      3. They are unstable and not to be trusted
         a. They have no anchor in the storms of life
         b. Consider the contrasts between people of faith and doubters
   B. *There Is a Great Dividing Day Coming (v. 5)*
      1. Sinners and saints will be separated
      2. Blessings await those who have placed faith in God
         a. Sorrow is coming to those who have rejected Christ
         b. What does the future hold for you?
      3. Wise ones turn from their sins to the Savior
      4. Make the choice that assures heaven for you
   C. *The Lord Knows the Way of the Righteous (v. 6)*
      1. There is no uncertainty for those who trust in Him
      2. How certain are you?

III. Conclusion
    A. *Settle This Eternal Question Today*
        1. Doubts bring distress
        2. Faith brings peace
    B. *The Lord Knows the Way of the Righteous*
    C. *The Way of the Ungodly Will Perish*

Robbing God

Malachi 3:8–12

I. Introduction
   A. *A Question*
      1. There are many perplexing questions in life
      2. Malachi records a question from God
   B. *A Question About God Being Robbed*
      1. Confusion about this strange question
      2. Why was this strange question being raised?
   C. *This Is a Question About God Being Robbed*
      1. Will a man rob God?
      2. The people were holding back on giving
      3. No wonder the people were charged with robbing God

II. Body
   A. *How Serious Is Robbing God?*
      1. These people were told they were cursed for robbing God
         a. Holding back from giving is very serious
         b. This was a charge against the whole nation
      2. Clearly, holding back on giving to God grieves Him
         a. This was no small transgression
         b. It involved both tithes and offerings
   B. *What Could Be Done to Right This Wrong? (v. 10)*
      1. Proper donations to God must be made
         a. This giving must begin immediately
         b. To tithe is to give 10 percent of income to the Lord
         c. Offerings are gifts above the tithe
      2. Increased income would result in greater blessings
         a. God promised to open the windows of heaven to givers
         b. This generosity would bring greater blessings
         c. Personal blessings to many givers have proven this true
   C. *What Would Be the Public Reaction to New Blessings? (vv. 11–12)*
      1. Others would notice the increase of God's blessings

2. The land would produce abundantly
3. Neighboring nations would witness God's provision
   a. They would call these giving people blessed
   b. God would prove that He keeps His promises
4. Many would conclude that increased giving means greater blessings

III. Conclusion

A. *Those Who Give Generously Receive*
B. *Who Will Prove That God's Promises Are True?*
C. *Let's Give Our Way to God's Blessings*

How to Receive More Than We Give

Luke 6:38

I. Introduction
A. *Words from Jesus About Giving and Receiving*
1. God intends that His people be generous givers
2. Jesus revealed a plan for receiving more than we give
B. *Is It Right to Expect Our Giving to Make Us Receivers?*
1. Let Jesus answer this frequently asked question (v. 38)
2. "Give, and it shall be given unto you"
   a. Here is a guarantee from the Lord that givers become receivers
   b. Consider also the quantities given and received
3. Givers receive more than they give
4. The Lord's description of the good measure in return
   a. Pressed down, shaken together, and running over
   b. Those who would receive in abundance should give abundantly

II. Body
A. *John Bunyan's Famous Quote About Generosity*
1. "A man there was, though some did think him mad; The more he cast away, the more he had."
2. Bunyan evidently wrote his quote from experience
   a. His years in Bedford jail proved his investment in time paid off
   b. He believed his giving produced his receiving
B. *Our Lord's Guarantee of "the Same Measure"*
1. Your receiving will equal or exceed your giving
   a. "The same measure that ye mete" is significant
   b. God controls the scales and makes them balance
2. Stinginess results in a poverty of blessing
3. Generosity guarantees increased blessings
4. Notice the compressing of receipts over donations

         a. Givers now move into the good measure category
         b. Their possessions are pressed down and shaken together
         c. The total report of their receipts is: "running over"

  C. *The Old and New Testaments Agree on Giving and Receiving*
      1. The more we give to God and invest in His work, the more we receive
      2. The less we surrender to the Lord and His work, the less we receive
      3. Giving and receiving are investments that pay high dividends
         a. The question is not "How much can we keep?"
         b. It is "How much can we give to honor and bless others?"

III. Conclusion
  A. *Let's Increase Our Giving Expecting Blessings*
  B. *Our Lord Guarantees Rewards to Those Who Invest Wisely*
  C. *Will We Become the Giving Church God Wants Us to Be?*
  D. *Only If We Invest for Eternity*

Secret Prayer

Matthew 6:6–8

I. Introduction

    A. *Prayer Is the Believer's Source of Power*
        1. We all face problems too big for us to solve
        2. We're confronted by enemies too strong for us to overcome
        3. Secret prayer is the source of power for all occasions
    B. *Instructions from Jesus for Powerful Praying*
        1. The place to pray: "Enter into thy closet"
        2. Powerful praying is private: "Shut the door"

II. Body

    A. *Secret Prayer Involves Just Two*
        1. The place of prayer is for the Lord and you
        2. You know His love will see you through
            a. No problem looms beyond His care
            b. You're not alone: He'll meet you there
        3. God has promised He'll provide
        4. He's always on the believer's side
        5. Secret prayers bring public answers (v. 6)
            a. Need the best? Conceive it!
            b. Need perfect rest? Believe it!
    B. *Secret Prayer Isn't Advertised (v. 5)*
        1. There is no pride in secret prayer
            a. Secret prayer doesn't cultivate a reputation
            b. Secret prayer doesn't promote hypocrisy
            c. Secret prayer doesn't keep earthly rewards
        2. There are no accolades in secret prayer
            a. Few praise those praying secretly
            b. No one is elected to pray alone or quietly
        3. Secret prayer touches the heart of God
            a. He answers personal, private prayer
            b. Heavenly rewards await those who pray secretly
    C. *Secret Prayer Cannot Be Programmed*
        1. Secret prayer springs from a quiet heart
        2. Secret prayers can bring awakenings to churches

3. Secret prayers can bring hope to hushed hospital halls
4. Secret prayers can restore love to troubled families
5. Secret prayers can bring blessings and glory to God

III. Conclusion
    A. *Secret Prayers Can Bring Revival*
    B. *Who Will Find a Secret Place to Pray for Our Church?*

A Mother's Plea for Her Son

1 Kings 17:17–24

I. **Introduction**
   A. *A Mother Who Has Suffered Great Loss*
      1. She is a widow, so has already lost her husband
      2. She is a woman of faith and has ministered to Elijah
      3. Now her only son has died, and grief is consuming her
   B. *Where Can a Mother Turn When in Need?*
      1. This grieving mother turns to a man of God
      2. Elijah shows her compassion and ministers to her need
      3. He takes her son in his arms and sets a miracle in motion

II. **Body**
   A. *Elijah Prepares to Pray and the Answer Is on Its Way*
      1. The prophet takes the widow's son into a loft and talks to God
         a. He asks God why the widow's son has died (vv. 19–20)
         b. He wants to know God's purpose in the widow's heartache
         c. He prays for healing for the widow's son (v. 21)
         d. See how specific Elijah is in his praying (v. 21)
      2. The Lord heard the earnest prayer of Elijah (v. 22)
         a. "Let this child's soul come into him again" (v. 21)
         b. This is a prayer for resurrection by the living God
      3. Elijah's announcement of victory
         a. The child is delivered to his mother alive
         b. What good news for this rejoicing mother! (v. 23)
   B. *The Scene of Victory and Vindication (v. 24)*
      1. The vindication of Elijah
         a. "By this I know that thou art a man of God"
         b. All doubts about Elijah's character and power evaporated

81

    2. The vindication of God's wisdom, power, and love
       a. The word of God was in His servant's mouth
       b. Everything Elijah had said was true
  C. *We Can Trust God During Tough Times*
    1. No problem is too difficult for God to solve
    2. No tragedy is too trying for God to bring peace
    3. The servants of God are equipped for every situation
       a. We can trust God to give wisdom to His servants
       b. God's power is sufficient when hope seems gone
    4. Faith brings victory on the darkest day

III. Conclusion
  A. *Trying Times Yield to Truth*
  B. *What Difficult Problem Do You Face Today?*
  C. *Make Every Adversity an Adventure*

What to Do with Our Burdens

Psalm 55:22–23

I. **Introduction**
    A. *We Are All Familiar with Burdens*
        1. We may have family burdens
        2. We may have financial burdens
        3. We may have burdens related to fears
    B. *Our Burdens Have Not Taken God by Surprise*
        1. This is a great anchor for our faith
        2. Our tomorrows are known to God before they arrive
        3. Solutions to our problems are awaiting our acceptance

II. **Body**
    A. *God's Great Invitation*
        1. We can cast our burdens on the Lord
        2. He is waiting to receive all our trials and temptations
        3. God's love is stronger than any enemy we face
            a. Why then should we worry or fret?
            b. No trial has overcome a believer yet
    B. *God's Blessed Boundaries for Believers*
        1. Consider God's boundary of love
        2. Every trial must pass through these blessed boundaries
        3. Remember God's boundary of grace
        4. Don't forget God's boundary of compassion
        5. Expect God's boundaries of blessing to keep you safe
    C. *God's Great Mission Cancels Satan's Permission*
        1. We are safe in the arms of our loving Lord
        2. We live in the circle of God's care
        3. No enemy will be permitted to harm us
        4. God has a wonderful plan for us
            a. Why should we worry?
            b. The psalmist's statement of peace: "I will trust in thee."

III. Conclusion
   A. *Some Are Headed for Destruction*
      1. The future of the wicked is fearful
      2. Judgment awaits those who reject salvation
      3. Let's be sure we're not in the company of the lost
   B. *Great Days Await Those Who Trust in the Lord*
      1. In whom have you placed your trust?
      2. Join the psalmist in declaring your faith is in God
   C. *The Lord Will Never Fail or Forsake You*

Rest for Weary Souls

I. Introduction
   A. An Invitation from Jesus: "Come unto me" (v. 28)
1. Here is an invitation to the weary
2. A loving call to all who are exhausted from their work

   B. Our Lord Knows the Limit of Our Endurance
1. Faith perceives that our fatigue is known by the Lord
2. Workers in the Lord's harvest can be sure of their Master's concern
3. Rest awaits those who respond to His loving call

II. Body
   A. The Lord's Description of His Call
1. "Take my yoke upon you, and learn of me" (v. 29)
   a. This invitation from Jesus guarantees equality in service
   b. Christians become partners with their Lord in His work
2. Day by day we learn more of God's gentle love
   a. The humble Savior makes serving Him a joy
   b. Why should anyone hold back from full surrender?

   B. Laboring with Jesus Enlists Us in a Divine Call
1. This is heavenly work in a troubled world
2. We become partners in a divine effort to win the lost

   C. The Mystery of Serving with Joy
1. Here is service that brings untold blessings
2. In God's service, we are busy but blessed
   a. Serving God brings great satisfaction
   b. Fatigue fades because such service is joy
3. The Lord's yoke is easy and His burden is light because . . .
   a. He supplies the strength
   b. His work is joy
   c. Serving God is the most fulfilling work in the world

III. Conclusion
  A. *Responding to God's Call Is a Great Opportunity*
    1. We receive the rewards of obedience to the will of God
    2. Our labor will bring us eternal blessings
    3. Why then should we hold back from giving our all?
  B. *Rest for the Soul Is Our Greatest Opportunity*
    1. Earthly gains cannot compare with heavenly rewards
    2. Andrew Murray: "Rest for the soul: such was the first promise with which the Savior sought to win the heavy-laden sinner."
  C. *The Rest Jesus Gives Will Last Forever*
  D. *The Best Is Yet to Come*

Onward and Upward

Philippians 3:12–14; 1 Corinthians 3:12–14

I. Introduction
A. *Paul's Prayer for Progress*
1. He admits imperfections
   a. "Not as though I had already attained"
   b. He makes no claim of being perfect
2. Paul kept pressing on, as should we
   a. He wanted to be more and more like Jesus
   b. How do our goals compare to those of Paul?
B. *Weakness Wins the Prize*
1. Weak ones must rest completely in their strong Lord
   a. Faith compensates for our feebleness
   b. Eternity will reveal the power of God working through weak ones
2. God's plan declares that the best is yet to come

II. Body
A. *The Builder and His Materials*
1. The Lord has a plan for every life
2. He also promises materials for us to use to fulfill His plan
3. Faith provides a foundation on which we can build
B. *We Choose Which Building Materials to Use (1 Cor. 3:12–14)*
1. Some wisely choose valuable materials
   a. Gold, silver, and precious stones
   b. These speak of a building of lasting value
2. Some choose temporary and trivial building materials
   a. Wood, hay, and straw (or stubble)
   b. This building will disappoint the builders and their Lord
3. We should examine our building materials often
4. We're called to construct lives, so we must be careful builders
C. *Rewards Await Those Who Build with Care*
1. Good builders build up the lives of others

    2. They set an example of trusting in God always
    3. Their purpose is living to the glory of God
    4. The rewards given to these builders will last forever

III. Conclusion
    A. *Onward-and-Upward People Build Up Their Church*
        1. These builders impact their families to live for Christ
        2. The neighborhoods where they live are changed
    B. *These People Live for the Glory of God*
    C. *May Their Numbers Continually Increase*

God's Great Plan for Growth

Colossians 2:6–7

I. **Introduction**
   A. *Believing Is Just the Beginning*
      1. Salvation begins with believing
      2. Faith opens the door to eternal life
   B. *Grace and Faith Make Multiplied Miracles Possible*
      1. Grace and faith are unearned gifts from God (Eph. 2:8–9)
      2. These great gifts make Christian growth a normal experience

II. **Body**
   A. *Imagine Our Church Filled with Growing Christians*
      1. Visualize this congregation on the move for God
         a. See a company of Christians without bitterness and anger
         b. Imagine a church full of people who care for the lost
         c. Think of the difference we could make in the community
      2. How can this miracle take place?
         a. We must get back to beginnings
         b. "As ye have therefore received Christ Jesus the Lord"
         c. This was Paul's call to return to the starting place
         d. "So walk ye in him" (Col. 2:6)
      3. Let faith soar and the best will be yet to come
   B. *Paul's Call for Growing in Three Directions*
      1. Growing through walking like Jesus (v. 6)
         a. Christ is our perfect example
         b. Walking like Jesus will draw others to Him
      2. Growing through being rooted in Jesus (v. 7)
         a. Increasing daily in our knowledge of Him
         b. Choosing to follow His example
      3. Growing daily: being established in the faith
   C. *Demonstrating Growth Through Thanksgiving*
      1. We should be ever praising, never pouting

      a. We are to demonstrate faith, not fear
      b. We are to be glorying in grace, not grumbling
         and growling
   2. We should be always triumphant, never troubled
      over trifles
   3. Christians should be the most positive people on
      earth

III. Conclusion
   A. How Does the World See Us?
   B. How Will They React to What They See?
   C. Will We Be Effective Witnesses for Our Lord?
      1. We live in a needy world
      2. Does this needy world see Christ in us?
      3. How can we be more effective in our witness for
      Him?

Joshua Graduates

I. Introduction

A. *Why Joshua Is Remembered*
1. He fought the battle of Jericho
2. The walls came tumblin' down

B. *Other Important Facts About Joshua*
1. He became Moses' assistant when young
2. He accompanied Moses to Mt. Sinai
3. He was chosen by Moses as one of twelve scouts of Canaan
4. His name is the Old Testament equivalent of "Jesus"

C. *Joshua's Graduation Day: He Must Become Leader of His People*
1. The greatest challenge of his life
2. There are many graduations in life
   a. Those from school
   b. Those from other experiences in life
   c. Final graduation

II. Body

A. *God Has a Plan for Joshua's Life (vv. 1–2)*
1. Joshua had been born in Egypt as a slave
   a. His future seemed to lie in slavery
   b. God had a plan that went beyond Joshua's prospects
2. Joshua was delivered from slavery
   a. A man named Moses came into his life
   b. This man would impact Joshua for God
   c. The Passover: deliverance by blood . . . the gospel
3. Joshua became Moses' assistant
4. God's plan for Joshua began to unfold
5. Moses died and Joshua became the leader
6. God has a plan for your life
   a. A good plan—one that goes beyond your dreams
   b. A plan that goes beyond aptitude tests
   c. A plan you can get in on by total surrender

    B. *God Gave Joshua Promises to Accompany His Plan*
       (vv. 3–5)
      1. A promise of blessing (v. 3)
      2. A promise of enlargement (v. 4)
      3. A promise of His presence (v. 5)
      4. A promise for the tough times
        a. Being in the will of God doesn't mean missing
          tough times
        b. But in tough times, we have His promises to
          sustain us
    C. *God's Word Was to Be the Secret of Joshua's Success*
       (vv. 6–8)
      1. No success apart from taking in God's Word
        regularly
        a. God's Word to build faith
        b. God's Word enables us to overcome temptation
        c. God's Word to meet us in times of defeat (Josh.
          7:4–10)
        d. God's Word to bring about Christian growth
      2. Consider the blessed man of Psalm 1
      3. Is God's Word a part of your daily life?
      4. Do you long to study and learn from it?

III. Conclusion
    A. *Summary and Application*
    B. *Surrender to Christ and Commence with Life*

All You Need to Know to Grow

1 Corinthians 3:1–5

I. **Introduction**
   A. *God's Great Plan for Your Life: Birth, Growth, and Maturity*
      1. But many believers never seem to develop
      2. We have churches full of spiritual babies
      3. This is not a new problem (1 Cor. 3:1–5)
   B. *What Are the Indications of Spiritual Infancy?*
      1. Griping instead of gratefulness
      2. Argument instead of action
      3. Following men instead of the Master
   C. *How Can One Get On with Growth?*

II. **Body**
   A. *You Must Be Born Again (John 3:1–21)*
      1. No birth, no growth
      2. Many try to imitate Christian maturity without being born again
      3. Nicodemus learns that he must be born again
         a. A very religious man, a ruler of the Jews
         b. How surprised and confused he was by our Lord's reply
         c. You may be very religious but lost
      4. Born again through faith in Christ (John 3:16)
   B. *You Must Learn How to Feed Yourself (1 Peter 2:2)*
      1. We need proper food for proper growth
      2. So much available today that is not wholesome
         a. News with all its violence
         b. Constant entertainment with questionable plots and presentations
      3. Each believer must develop a daily devotional time
         a. Start the day with God and His Word
         b. Take time for thanksgiving and prayer
         c. Use helpful devotionals
         d. Find faith builders for each day
   C. *You Must Learn to Allow Others to Feed You (Heb. 10:25)*

    1. The importance of the local church (Eph. 4:11–16)
      a. Church attendance is vital to Christian growth
      b. We need the pastor and teachers to feed us
      c. We need Christian fellowship to encourage us
      d. The ordinances of the church are experiences in obedience
      e. Opportunities for service enable us to grow strong
    2. Read faith-building books
    3. Listen to good music
    4. Expect the Holy Spirit to speak through others
    5. Seeing Christ in the lives of brothers and sisters in Christ

D. *You Must Learn to Walk (Gal. 5:16)*
    1. Walk in the Spirit
      a. Grieve not the Spirit (Eph. 4:30)
      b. Quench not the Spirit (1 Thess. 5:19)
    2. How to walk
      a. Walk in newness of life (Rom. 6:4)
      b. Walk by faith (2 Cor. 5:7)
      c. Walk worthy of the Lord (Col. 1:10)
      d. Walk circumspectly (Eph. 5:15)
      e. Walk in love (Eph. 5:2)
      f. Walk as children of light (Eph. 5:8)

E. *You Must Learn How to Reproduce Spiritually*
    1. *Born to Reproduce* by Dawson Trotman, founder of the Navigators
    2. God's plan for reproducing: going, sowing, weeping, reaping (Ps. 126:5–6)
    3. Organized outreach; individual witnessing

III. Conclusion
    A. *Peter's Plea: "Grow in grace, and in the knowledge of our Lord and Savior Christ" (2 Peter 3:18)*
    B. *Growth for You and Me*

The Conversion of Saul to Paul

Acts 9

I. Introduction
    A. *Great News at Any Conversion*
        1. Joy in the presence of the angels of God
        2. Joy in the hearts of believers
    B. *How Important When It Becomes Personal*

II. Body
    A. *The Question of Conviction: "Why persecutest thou me?" (Acts 9:4)*
        1. First introduction to Saul
            a. Prayers for Saul
            b. The reaching of this man
        2. Saul the intellectual
            a. Maybe the greatest mind
            b. "Not many wise" (1 Cor. 1:26)
        3. God sent an experience to Saul to make him aware of his sin
        4. What must God send your way?
    B. *The Question of Conversion: "Who art thou, Lord?" (Acts 9:5)*
        1. The question that really asks, "What is the real answer to life?"
        2. Saul, who had sat the feet of Gamaliel
        3. Saul, who had been a leader in religion
        4. Saul did not expect the answer he received: "I am Jesus"
            a. Jesus, whom he had scorned
            b. Jesus, whose life and death seemed an insult to his intelligence
            c. Jesus, whom he had come to resent
            d. Jesus, whose followers he despised
    C. *The Question of Consecration: "Lord, what wilt Thou have me to do? (Acts 9:6)*
        1. Here is a statement of surrender
        2. Now history is made: Saul will be used of God to change the world
        3. Saul to be God's servant

III. Conclusion
    A. What This Experience Says to You
    B. Let the Lord Meet You Where You Are

"And Peter"

Matthew 26:69–75; Mark 16:7

I. Introduction
A. *The Criticized Disciple*
1. Most condemned disciple outside of Judas
2. Used often for a multitude of illustrations
B. *Yet a Favorite Disciple*
1. His enthusiasm
2. His bravery and devotion
C. *Peter and His Backsliding: The Dark Hour of His Life*

II. Body
A. *Peter's Faith and His Following (Matt. 26:33, 58)*
1. I will not be offended (v. 33)
2. Flesh/Spirit (Matt. 26:41; Rom. 7:19–25; 1 Cor. 10:12; Gal. 5:17)
3. Abraham and Lot, Joseph and Potiphar's wife
4. Samson, David, and Solomon
5. Flee to Jesus; get close to Him
B. *Peter's Fellowship and His Forgetfulness (vv. 69–75)*
1. Moving among bad company
2. Bad company makes one forget Christ
3. Prodigal son and when he remembered
4. The rich man in hell
5. Psalm 1:1
6. You are not stronger than Peter
C. *Peter's Fear and His Falsehoods (vv. 69–75)*
1. "The fear of man bringeth a snare" (Prov. 29:25)
2. Falsehoods in life because of fear of man
3. Denied Jesus with an oath

III. Conclusion
A. *Peter's Great Remorse*
1. He wept bitterly
2. The legend of the following years
B. *The Great Forgiving Savior*
1. Jesus' prayer for Peter (Luke 22:31–32)
2. Christ's words after the resurrection (John 21:15–17)

The First Revival in the Church

Acts 2:41–47

I. **Introduction**
  A. *Communion and Revival*
    1. Walter Boldt: Revival is "God at work, restoring His Church to health."
    2. Charles Finney: Revival is "the renewal of the first love of Christians, resulting in the awakening and conversion of sinners to God."
  B. *The First and Twenty-First Centuries*
    1. Christians a tiny minority
    2. God's prophetic clock running swiftly
  C. *The First Revival: Church Born in Revival. Why? What Made the Difference?*

II. **Body**
  A. *They Had a Fresh Experience with Christ*
    1. A group of failures, unpromising individuals
    2. The commission they had received
    3. Not long before they had stood at the cross
      a. They had seen prophecies fulfilled
      b. They saw themselves as they were
      c. They saw Christ as their sacrifice
    4. They were also convinced He had risen
    5. They expected His return
  B. *They Were on Fire for Christ*
    1. "Cloven tongues like as of fire" (v. 3)
    2. The fire of new converts
    3. The world needs to see a church on fire
      a. Not just fundamental: on fire
      b. Not just sound in doctrine (may be sound asleep)
      c. Not just gospel preaching: going
      d. Not just missionary-minded; must be missionary in practice
    4. The scary word to Laodicea
  C. *They Had Found True Fellowship in Christ*
    1. This group, once divided, now love one another
    2. Note the basis of their fellowship

       a. The apostles' doctrine: truth
       b. The breaking of bread: Communion
       c. Prayer: what communion in prayer!
    3. Blessed be the tie that binds our hearts in Christian love

III. Conclusion
    A. *What Is God Doing in Your Life?*
    B. *How Fresh Is Your Experience?*

The Lord's Prayer on Father's Day

Matthew 6:9–13

I. **Introduction**
   *What Easy Father's Day Lessons Are Found in This
   Prayer?*

II. **Body**
   A. *It Speaks of the Father (v. 9)*
      1. Maybe we best understand our heavenly Father
         after becoming earthly fathers . . . the giving of His
         Son
      2. Our loving Father in heaven
      3. How much the Bible has to say about the Father
         a. He sees the sparrow fall
         b. He feeds the birds
         c. He longs to take away our fears
         d. He sent His Son
      4. We become His children by faith in Jesus (John
         1:12)
   B. *It Speaks of the Future (v. 10)*
      1. "Thy kingdom come"
      2. Do you tire of all the crime and sorrow of this
         world?
      3. Are you fed up with the violence and headlines?
      4. Are you discouraged about developments in the
         nations?
      5. There is a better day coming (Isa. 11)
   C. *It Speaks of Food (v. 11)*
      1. Our heavenly Father provides our daily bread
         a. He gives the strength to work
         b. He provides jobs
         c. He has His hand in our financial matters
      2. Have you been thankful today for food?
   D. *It Speaks of Forgiveness*
      1. What a good word it is!
      2. We can forgive because we have been forgiven
      3. God's love is proven because He forgives
      4. If you wonder if the Father loves you, remember the
         cross!

E. *It Speaks of Freedom*
   1.   All sin enslaves
   2.   Yielding to temptation brings bondage
   3.   Many lives ruined by yielding to temptation
   4.   But our Lord is able to deliver us from temptation
        (1 Cor. 10:13)
F. *It Ends with Assurance About Forever*
   1.   He is the God of forever
   2.   We are tied to time
   3.   He knows all about the issues of eternity
   4.   Are you ready for eternity?

III. Conclusion
   A. *The Lord's Prayer on Father's Day*
   B. *Prepared for Time and Eternity*

Watching Jesus Die!

Luke 23:46

I. **Introduction**
  A. *Palm Sunday (Matt. 21:1–11)*
      1. The crowds, the branches, and the cry
      2. From crown Him to crucify Him
  B. *From There to the Cross*
      1. John 10:10–18: Laying down his life to take it again
      2. The garden, the judgment, the scourging, and the cross
  C. *The Calvary Road: The Representative Crowds*
      1. The faithful few, Peter, and Joseph of Arimathaea
      2. The priests, the Pharisees, and the soldiers
  D. *Watching Jesus Die! What This Must Have Made Them Realize*
      1. His tenderness ("Father, forgive them. . . ." "Woman, behold thy son")
      2. His compassion for sinners ("Today, thou shalt be with me . . .")
      3. His agony ("My God, my God . . ." "I thirst")
      4. His purpose: a work to do ("It is finished")
      5. The final words as Jesus dies ("Into thy hands I commit my spirit")

II. **Body**
  A. *Every Man Possesses a Spirit*
      1. The emphasis upon the physical at the crucifixion
      2. The sale for silver, the whipping, the nails, the thorns, the blood
      3. "His blood be on us, and on our children" (Matt. 27:25)
      4. The spiritual omitted from their thoughts:
          a. Not on the minds of the soldiers gambling there
          b. Even the priests had degraded the truth into formal religion
          c. The thieves had only been concerned with what they got
      5. Have you forgotten the spiritual in your life?

B. *Every Man's Spirit Will Consciously Exist After the Body Is Dead*
   1. The rich man and Lazarus; the reality of hell
   2. Moses at the Mount of Transfiguration (Matt. 17)
   3. The ministry of Christ while His body was in the grave (1 Peter 3:19)
   4. Revelation 6; note that the souls come out of tribulation
   5. Where will you be five minutes after you die?
C. *It Is Possible for Every Man to Prepare and Know the Destination of His Spirit After Death*
   1. Note the confidence and victory of the Savior
   2. Remember the words of Jesus to the thief (Luke 23:43)
   3. Remember John 14
   4. See this carried through in the church (Acts 7:54–60)
   5. Do you know the destination of your spirit after death?

III. **Conclusion**
   A. *Effect on Those Who Watched Jesus Die!*
   B. *What Will Be the Effect on You?*

Jesus Takes Barabbas's Place

Matthew 27:16–26

I. Introduction
  A. *The Most Uncomfortable Man in Jerusalem*
   1. Pilate is under pressure from the Jews
   2. The dream of his wife: have nothing to do with Him
   3. Pilate's struggle to release Jesus
  B. *Pilate's Great Question (v. 22)*
   1. His question should be your question today
   2. Finally decides to resolve it by washing his hands, choosing neutrality
  C. *Decides to Release Barabbas and Crucify Jesus*

II. Body
  A. *The Contrast Between Jesus and Barabbas (vv. 16–19)*
   1. The choice between the natural and the spiritual man
   2. The superficial differences that confuse men
   3. Consider the differences that count with God
   4. Let us consider Barabbas
    a. He was a murderer and guilty of insurrection
    b. He was basically unhappy and so became anti-social in conduct
    c. But was he really different?
     (1) Thousands had murdered before him
     (2) Millions had followed the leaders of riots and insurrection
   5. Each generation's desire to be different than the one before
    a. Clothes, hair, new things
    b. But there is nothing new under the sun (Eccl. 1)
   6. Youths and adults, please notice the difference. The real difference lies with choosing between sin and righteousness in any generation
  B. *The Choice Between Jesus and Barabbas (vv. 20–24)*
   1. Pilate offers the crowd a choice between Jesus and Barabbas
   2. "Whom will ye that I release unto you?" (v. 17)

3. Their choice between
   a. Wickedness and righteousness
   b. Sin and holiness
   c. Darkness and light
4. How they make their choice (v. 20)
   a. They are influenced by others
   b. Many will be lost because others influenced them
5. What will be your choice today?

C. *The Consequences of the Choice Between Jesus and Barabbas (vv. 25–26)*
1. The consequences for the people
2. The consequence for Jesus
   a. Scourged and delivered by Pilate to be crucified
   b. Christ died for Barabbas
3. The consequences for Barabbas: set free—the perfect type of substitutionary atonement
4. The consequences for the Jews (v. 25)

III. Conclusion
A. *What Will You Do with Jesus?*
B. *You Can Be Free from Sin and Death*

Revival

Acts 4:31–33

I. **Introduction**
   A. *A Message About Revival*
      1. A word used often in our day
      2. Most Christians agree that we need revival
      3. Some even feel the nation will die without it
      4. Few expect it
   B. *The Urgent Need for Revival Now!*
      1. The conditions of our day: you know them
      2. The shortness of the time: prophetic fulfillment

II. **Body**
   A. *What Revival Is*
      1. The meaning is to make live again
      2. Something deeper than a week of meetings with an evangelist or singing group
         a. Yet that is the usual thought about revival
         b. Ads: Revival Will Begin —, Revival Will End —,
      3. Revival is specifically the business of Christians
         a. Has to do with bringing back life that was there
         b. Cannot be the experience of the world
         c. Cannot be legislated, decreed, or voted on
         d. Walter Boldt: Revival is "God at work, restoring His Church to health." This may be true of the whole body of Christ, a single church, or an individual Christian
      4. If you are not saved, you do not need revival; you need salvation
      5. Who needs revival?
         a. A Christian who remembers a better day
         b. A Christian who has lost the joy of his salvation
         c. A Christian who has become callous or cold or critical
         d. A Christian who has become weak or wanton or worldly
   B. *What Revival Does*
      1. Revival revitalizes prayer: "And when they prayed . . ."

    a. What Peter would have done before revival: despaired

    b. What Thomas would have done before revival: doubted

    c. What the women would have done before revival: religious acts

    d. Now under tense conditions, they pray powerfully

    e. The blessed cycle of prayer in every great work

2. Revival cleanses the church of divisions and differences

    a. "Were of one heart and one soul"

    b. Love in action; petty grudges fade away

    c. Old wounds healed; forgiveness flows freely

3. Christians become power-conscious instead of problem-conscious

    a. Searching for problems to air

    b. What the Lord is doing—or the Devil

4. Revival produces powerful witness (v. 33)

    a. Some churches quarrel and fight; others are just mutual admiration societies; both are wrong

    b. If not a greater concern for souls, we have failed

C. *When Revival Starts*

1. Revival starts when one or more people get thoroughly right with God and one another

2. Revival starts when you want it to start. "Send a revival, start the work in me"—from the hymn "Cleanse Me" by Edwin Orr

III. Conclusion

A. *Do You Really Want Revival?*

B. *Rodney "Gypsy" Smith: "Go home. Lock yourself in your room. Kneel down in the middle of the floor, and with a piece of chalk, draw a circle around yourself. There, on your knees, pray fervently and brokenly that God would start a revival within that chalk circle."*

America: Her Greatest Enemy, Her Greatest Asset, and Her Greatest Opportunity

Proverbs 14:34

I. **Introduction**
   A. *Give Me Liberty or Give Me Death*
      1. The cry that roused our forefathers to fight for liberty
      2. Perhaps not since that time has America stood so close to that choice
   B. *Today I Want to Thank God for America*
      1. Certainly raised up by God for His purposes, including missionary activity
      2. May she be free until Jesus comes!
   C. *America and the World in Great Peril*

II. **Body**
   A. *America—Her Greatest Enemy (Isa. 14:12)*
      1. "Thou . . . which didst weaken the nations"
      2. America's enemies
      3. America's real enemy is Satan
         a. He discounts the importance of God's word (Gen. 3)
         b. He discounts the reality of God's judgments (moral decline)
         c. He distorts the value of God's blessings (Exod. 32)
            (1) Israel in crossing the Red Sea
            (2) Israel in worship of the golden calf
         d. He displays the so-called benefits of sin
      4. America weakened by sin
   B. *America—Her Greatest Asset (Prov. 14:34)*
      1. Righteousness exalts a nation
      2. Amid the sin and licentiousness there is a godly remnant
      3. Righteousness and its value to a nation
         a. Righteousness brings wealth and blessing from above (Deut. 28)
         b. Righteousness that withholds the judgment of God (Lot)

       c. Righteousness that withholds the rise of the Antichrist

    4. For the elect's sake (Matt. 24)

C. *America—Her Greatest Opportunity (Rev. 5:9)*

    1. The scene from heaven: the reason they were there

    2. The land of opportunity

    3. The opportunity to hear, to heed, to herald the gospel

    4. Make it personal, plain, and precious

    5. The eternal value of salvation

III. Conclusion

A. *The Tragedy of America Being Lost*

    1. The Bible institutes and the missionary work

    2. The world in slavery

B. *The Tragedy of Being Lost in America*

    1. Dying of thirst at the spring

    2. Be saved today; Jesus' warning

The Ruler of the Waves

Mark 4:35–41

I. **Introduction**
   A. *The Story of One of Christ's Greatest Miracles*
      1. When Jesus made the elements obey Him
      2. Man with all his knowledge and power today can't control storms
         a. Tornadoes, hurricanes, etc.
         b. The swirling clouds and the supernatural Savior
   B. *Come to the Sea of Galilee*
      1. The parables, the multitude, and the authority
      2. Evening comes and the sun begins to set; the weary Savior
   C. *The Ruler of the Waves*

II. **Body**
   A. *The Statement (vv. 35–36): "Let us pass over unto the other side"*
      1. Note what happens as a result of that statement
         a. The disciples send the multitude away
         b. No questions asked as to the weather
         c. The late hour seemed no problem
      2. What that statement guaranteed
         a. That when the disciples got into the boat—Jesus would too
         b. That Jesus had business on the other side
         c. That the ship was absolutely unsinkable
      3. Note how similar that statement is to Christ's invitation to salvation
         a. The sea: the sea of life
         b. The other side: heaven
   B. *The Storm (vv. 37–38)*
      1. There arose a great storm of wind
         a. All was peaceful in the ship with Jesus
         b. Suddenly the storm was there and the waves beat high
      2. How quickly the storms of life descend
         a. All is moving smoothly, then suddenly there is some crisis: physical, financial, family

  b. It's a short distance from triumph to tears, the mount to the valley

 3. Notice these important facts

  a. Christians experience storms too

  b. Christians are sometimes weak in the storm

  c. Christians have a refuge in the storm

  d. Baffled and afraid, they call on Jesus

C. *The Savior (vv. 38–40)*

 1. "Carest thou not that we perish?"

  a. What a statement to make to Jesus!

  b. He came that men might not perish (John 3:16)

 2. The disciples thought He didn't care, or He wouldn't have allowed the storm, but that was not true

 3. Christ is not dead today; He is not just the God of yesterday

 4. Christ responds to their call

  a. He rises and rebukes the sea

  b. There is a great calm; He rebukes their fears

III. Conclusion

A. *Notice How Much More Jesus Means to Them: "What manner of man is this?"*

B. *Let Christ Calm Your Storms*

Members of the Body

1 Corinthians 12:12–31

I. Introduction
 A. *Dealing with a Delicate Subject*
  1. One upon which there is much disagreement
  2. One that should unite but instead divides
 B. *Don't Miss the Most Important Issue*
  1. Your need is not doctrine but deliverance
  2. It is not sectarian but salvation
  3. Make the gospel plain
 C. *Seeking to Make a Deep Truth Plain*

II. Body
 A. *Baptism into the Body of Christ (vv. 12–13)*
  1. The promise of baptism of the Holy Spirit (Matt. 3:11; John 1:26)
  2. The promise to the disciples (Acts 1:5)
   a. The fulfillment to the disciples
   b. Why different from our experience?
  3. The mystery of becoming a part of Christ's body
   a. Jesus' prayer for this (John 17:20–23)
   b. The mystery of a young couple becoming one (Eph. 5)
  4. Notice:
   a. This baptism that unites us is by the Spirit, not by water
   b. This baptism involves all Christians
   c. This baptism takes place at salvation (Rom. 8:9)
 B. *Diversity in the Body of Christ (vv. 14–18)*
  1. Made up of different races and faces
  2. Walking, hearing, seeing (vv. 15–17)
  3. How easy it is for us to fail here
  4. The two great dangers
   a. The danger of thinking we are not pleasing Christ unless we imitate someone else
   b. The danger of thinking other Christians are failing if they do not conform perfectly to our way (Phil. 2:1–8)
  5. "As it hath pleased him" (v. 18)

C. *Unity in the Body of Christ (vv. 19–27)*
   1. Notice that this unity is an organism, not an organization
      a. The drive for so-called Christian unity is wrongly based
      b. The Lord never prayed for nor planned for a super-church
   2. The ecumenical search for some document that will unite all Christianity will fail
      a. The same way that a scientist cannot build a man
      b. The letter kills; the Spirit gives life
   3. The importance of Christians to each other
   4. No schism in the body

III. **Conclusion**
   A. *The Bond That Builds the Body of Christ*
      1. Love that ties it all together
      2. Let us pray that such love will be ours
   B. *Read 1 Corinthians 13*

I Am Debtor

Romans 1:14–17

I. **Introduction**
   A. *Some Think the World Owes Them a Living*
      1. Laziness
      2. Grumbling when all is not going well
   B. *Paul Thought He Owed the World Something*
      1. God had rescued Paul from heartache and hell
      2. Paul ever sought to bring other men to the divine good news
   C. *"I Am Debtor"*

II. **Body**
   A. *Paul, the Man in Debt (v. 14)*
      1. A man in debt is a man who has received something
         a. In debt: a car, a home, food, service
         b. Paul has received something: salvation
      2. Paul's debt is not a debt of sin
         a. The first thought of many of us
         b. That debt paid at the cross; we never could pay it
      3. Paul's debt is a debt of gratitude
         a. Gratitude for having been saved
         b. Gratitude for God's grace toward him
   B. *To Whom Must Paul Pay His Debt?*
      1. To the Greeks and to the Barbarians, to the wise and the unwise
      2. Important to know where the debt must be paid
         a. The address on the envelope or the payment book
         b. Our debt of gratitude must be paid in service to men
      3. Illustrations of how this must be true
         a. The good news: God doesn't need it—men do
         b. Grace: God doesn't need it—men do
         c. Forgiveness: God doesn't need it—men do
      4. How to minister to the needs of Jesus
         a. His hunger—You'll find plenty who are hungry

      b. His heartache and tears—You'll find plenty in
         tears
      c. His wounds: many are hurt and bleeding now
      d. Inasmuch as ye have done it to the least of these
         (Matt. 25:40)
   5. Notice the scope of Paul's indebtedness
      a. Greeks and Barbarians: the cultured and the
         uncouth
      b. Wise and unwise: the educated and the ignorant
      c. Narrowing visions: we must keep widening our
         vision

C. *Paul Ready to Pay His Debt*
   1. "I am ready"; "So, as much as in me is . . ."
   2. Even though we are to "owe no man anything," we
      understand that we are to pay our debts as we are
      able
   3. Many conditions bring debts about, but ongoing
      debts are not understandable when one has the
      resources to pay them but will not
   4. Paul was willing and ready
   5. "So, as much as in me is": this is real consecration

III. Conclusion
   A. *Are You Ready?*
   B. *The Good Feeling of a Debt Paid*

Philip, the Dynamic Deacon

Acts 8:26–40

I. Introduction
A. *God's Giants Are Not Always So-Called Ministers*
   1. God has often been pleased to use others for His glory
   2. D. L. Moody, an untrained shoe salesman, shook two continents
   3. Billy Sunday, a professional baseball player turned influential evangelist
B. *Philip, the Dynamic Deacon*
   1. First introduced in Acts 6:5
   2. Philip turns out to be a great soul winner
   3. The greatest need of our day
C. *Secrets of This Layman for the Lord*

II. Body
A. *Philip Was in Tune with the Spirit of God (v. 29)*
   1. Philip and his success at Samaria (vv. 5–8)
   2. The Lord speaks supernaturally to Philip
   3. From the revival at Samaria to the desert
   4. Probably a great caravan with the eunuch's chariot in the midst of it
   5. Are you listening if God should send you to win another?
   6. God is definitely interested in definite results
   7. God sends His servants to prepare people
   8. So easy to put up our spiritual umbrellas and miss His will
B. *Philip's Tool Was the Word of God (v. 35)*
   1. The eunuch didn't find the answer at the services; now he searches the Scriptures—a good idea
   2. Reads as the horses jog along, invites Philip to help him
   3. Accept the servant God sends to guide you
   4. Philip began at the same Scripture
      a. Philip used the Word of God
      b. Philip preached unto him Jesus, the message of the Book

     5. It was Jesus who suffered and died for you
  C. *Philip's Target Was Salvation Through the Son of God*
      (v. 37)
     1. The eunuch's desire for baptism
     2. How easy for Philip to chalk up another convert
     3. The real aim was salvation, not just religion
     4. If you believe—Rom. 10:9
     5. The baptismal service in the desert

III. Conclusion
  A. *Push for Personal Witnessing and Soul Winning*
  B. *Listen to the Spirit, Use the Word of God, Focus on
     Jesus Christ*

From Strong Man to Slave

Judges 16

I. Introduction
   A. *Samson's Divine Birth: Promised to Manoah*
      1. The heartache ahead
      2. The possibilities
   B. *The Early Years and Great Strength*
      1. Godly parents, no habits of sin
      2. Lion killed, slay one thousand men, walks away with gates of Gaza, faster than foxes
      3. Samson and eye trouble
      4. Samson's false idea of playing with sin

II. Body
   A. *Sin Brings Recklessness (v. 17)*
      1. The evolution of sin
      2. First grass ropes, then weave locks into web, finally shaven
      3. Sin in secret brings sin in sight
      4. Secret now but reckless later
   B. *Sin Brings Powerlessness (v. 20)*
      1. The great lie of Satan and manliness
      2. The mighty Samson is powerless
      3. Power belongs unto God
   C. *Sin Brings Blindness (v. 21)*
      1. Samson's eyes poked out
      2. The tragic blindness of sin
      3. Blinded to the love and joy of Christ
      4. Blinded to the right
   D. *Sin Brings Slavery (v. 21)*
      1. The tragic picture of Samson the slave
      2. Blind, bald, and beaten
      3. Romans 6:1–13
      4. Don't become a slave to sin

III. Conclusion
   A. *The Call of Samson from His Slavery and Sin*
      1. God's answer and Samson's power
      2. The death of Samson

B. *The End of Samson's Life Could Have Been So
    Different*
C. *A Sinful Life Is a Wasted Life*

Bible Baptism

Matthew 3:13–17

I. Introduction
- A. *A Dangerous Subject*
  1. Church history shows that the time of baptism is often a time of persecution as well
  2. This is still often true on the mission field
- B. *A Greatly Misunderstood Subject*
  1. Some believe we are not to baptize with water at all
  2. The Church of Christ believes no salvation without it
  3. Some sprinkle, some pour, some immerse three times
  4. Some believe any Christian can baptize another; others believe only certain churchmen can baptize
- C. *Answering Questions About Baptism*

II. Body
- A. *Who Should Be Baptized?*
  1. There are many errors about this
     - a. Some baptize infants to keep them from hell
     - b. Some baptize as a first step in coming to God
     - c. Some are baptized for others, such as Mormons for the dead
  2. The Bible teaches that only the saved should be baptized
     - a. Acts 2:41: the converts in the New Testament church
     - b. Acts 10: Cornelius and his family
     - c. Acts 16:31–33: the jailor and his family
  3. The clincher—Acts 8:36–37: "If thou believest . . ."
- B. *How Should One Be Baptized?*
  1. Many unusual ideas about this
     - a. Sprinkling: several denominations
     - b. Pouring: also several
     - c. Immersion
  2. Immersion is proper because of the meaning of the word
     - a. *Baptizo*: to wash, dip, submerge

b. To immerse
3. Immersion because of the significance of the
    ordinance
    a. Communion pictures Christ's death
    b. Baptism pictures His burial and resurrection
        (Rom. 6:3–4)
4. Martin Luther: "I could wish that the baptized
    should be totally immersed, according to the
    meaning of the word and the signification of the
    mystery."
C. *Why Should One Be Baptized?*
    1. Baptism is following Jesus (Matt. 3:13–17)
    2. Baptism is obeying Jesus (Matt. 28:18–20)
    3. Baptism is public identification with Jesus (Acts
        2:41)
        a. The purpose of New Testament baptism
        b. The cost to the new converts
        c. Identification with the crucified, buried, and
            risen Christ

III. Conclusion
A. *Only the Saved Should Be Baptized*
B. *All Saved People Should Be Baptized by Immersion*
C. *Those Baptized Should See It as an Important
    Milestone in Their Christian Experience*

The Tribulation Period

Matthew 24:21-22

I. Introduction
- A. *One Hates to Expect a Time of Trouble*
  1. Far nicer only to think of the blessings foretold
  2. Easier to dwell on the rapture, the kingdom, and heaven
- B. *Yet the Bible Writers and Bible Students for Generations Have Seen a Time of Trouble in God's Word for This Earth*

II. Body
- A. *How Does the Bible Describe This Time of Trouble?*
  1. A time of indignation (Isa. 26:20-21; 34:1-4)
  2. A time of wrath (1 Thess. 5:1-10; Rev. 6:12-17; Rev. 16)
  3. A time of trouble (Jer. 30:7; Dan. 12:1)
  4. Great tribulation (Matt. 24:21-22)
  5. A time of distress of nations (Luke 21:25-26)
  6. A time of judgment (Rev. 14:7; 15:4; 19:2)
- B. *What Will Happen During This Tribulation Period?*
  1. A federation of states into the old Roman Empire (Dan. 2, 7)
  2. A rise of a political ruler of this empire who makes a covenant with Israel (Dan. 9:27)
  3. The formulation of a false religion under the false prophet (Rev. 13:11-18)
  4. The pouring out of the judgments under the seals (Rev. 6)
  5. The separation of the 144,000 witnesses (Rev. 7)
  6. The rise of God's two witnesses (Rev. 11)
  7. The terrible persecution of Israel (Rev. 12)
  8. The overthrow of a false professing church (Rev. 17-18)
  9. The battle of Armageddon (Rev. 16:16; 19:17-21)
  10. The destruction of the Beast and all his armies and the false prophet
- C. *How Does One Escape This Awful Time of Trouble?*
  1. There is a people not appointed to wrath (1 Thess. 5:9)

     a. This is the Achilles' heel of all
         post-tribulationists
     b. This is most definitely a time of wrath
  2. God's care for His bride
  3. You can move from wrath to redemption
  4. You can move from fear to faith; do so today
  5. Turn to Christ while you can

III. Conclusion
    A. Application and Call
    B. The Incentive and Joy of the Christian Life

God's Choice

1 Corinthians 1:26–31

I. Introduction
A. *The Situation at Corinth*
1. Divorce and remarriage
2. Confused services
3. Courts, Communion, collections
4. Moral problems and what to do
B. *The Cross—the Cure*
C. *God's Choice*
1. Some of the most surprising and interesting verses in Scripture
2. Corinthian confidence in worldly wisdom and talents

II. Body
A. *God Hath Chosen the Foolish to Confound the Wise (v. 27)*
1. Has reference to v. 18: the foolishness of the cross
2. Also to v. 21: the foolishness of preaching
   a. Heaping to themselves teachers who have itching ears
   b. The more distinguished, the less preaching
3. The old message is so strange to the worldly wise
4. The simple cannot miss it
   a. The saved are usually the less wise in worldly evaluation
   b. Sometimes those who are worldly wise realize their foolishness
B. *God Hath Chosen the Weak to Confound the Mighty (v. 27)*
1. In every age there are great works to be accomplished
2. God has chosen the weak to do His work
3. Remember his choice of David, Joseph, Gideon, and the mighty Midianites
4. The American colonies and the mighty British Empire
5. God's work and you

    C. God Hath Chosen the Base, the Despised, and the
       Things Which Are Not to Bring to Naught the Things
       That Are (v. 28)
      1. The base: the lowborn
        a. The background of many greatly used of God
        b. Christ became lowborn in the manger
      2. The despised
        a. God reaches into the gutter to save and use
           them
        b. Christ himself was despised and rejected of
           men
      3. The things which are not
        a. Things which may as well not exist
        b. God uses such things to His glory

III. Conclusion
    A. God's Plan
      1. To bring down the wise, the noble, the mighty
      2. Tied to the original fall of man
    B. God's Purpose
      1. That no flesh should glory in itself
      2. That all glorying might be in Christ

Saved to the Uttermost

Hebrews 7:25

I. Introduction
  A. *The Christian Message of Salvation*
    1. Luke 19:10; Rom. 10:9–13; Heb. 7:25
    2. Not just going to church, getting religion, living better, or joining the church
    3. God personally dealing with you
  B. *The Meaning of the Word*
    1. Deliverance, safety, and preservation
    2. Exod. 14:13; Ps. 3:8; Luke 19:9–10
  C. *"Saved to the Uttermost" (William J. Kirkpatrick, 1875): The Songwriter's Theme*

II. Body
  A. *What Will Salvation Do?*
    1. It is able to save to the uttermost
      a. Completely, finally, perfectly
      b. For all eternity
    2. It will change completely your destination
      a. Every man is on his way to a destination
      b. Israel apart from salvation was on her way back to slavery
    3. It will change completely your outlook on life
      a. The purpose of living (the case of Zacchaeus)
      b. The standard of values is changed
      c. Just passing through: laying up for the destination
    4. It will change completely your outlook upon death
      a. David: "I will both lay me down in peace, and sleep" (Ps. 4:8)
      b. Hebrews 2:15: delivered from the fear of death
  B. *To Whom Is Salvation Available?*
    1. Those who come to God by Jesus
    2. The single requirement
      a. A certain scholastic rating for college, but not so for salvation
      b. A certain trade to get employment, but not so

126

          for salvation

    c. A certain age to obtain privileges, but not so for salvation

    d. A certain credit rating to buy a home, but not so for salvation

    e. A certain position to join the club, but not so for salvation

  3. "Whosoever will" may come

  4. Explanation of the act of salvation

C. *How Can I Be Sure It Will Last?*

  1. "He ever liveth to make intercession for them"

  2. Putting my hand in His and letting Him lead me home

  3. Supposing . . .

    a. I live fifty years more, He ever liveth

    b. Temptation increases, He ever liveth

    c. I don't feel this way tomorrow, He ever liveth

III. Conclusion

  A. *What This Meant to the Hebrews*

  B. *What It Can Mean to You*

Why Hypocrites?

Matthew 13:24–30

I. Introduction
  A. *The Great Hypocrite Problem*
    1. Arises in almost every soul-winning effort
    2. The importance of the problem
       a. Stands out above all the saints of God
       b. Danger in lives of young Christians
  B. *What Is a Hypocrite?*
    1. The difference between a backslider and a hypocrite
    2. Difference between Peter and Judas
  C. *Why There Are Hypocrites in Churches Today*
    1. Christ anticipating the problem
    2. Knew what was in men

II. Body
  A. *Because Satan Closes the Eyes of Men to Realities (v. 25)*
    1. Satan's power to blind the minds of the lost (2 Cor. 4:4)
    2. The two classes of hypocrites
    3. The deceivers of others (Matt. 23:14)
       a. Eyes closed to the seriousness of eternal issues
       b. Eyes closed to the holy character of the Lord
    4. The deceivers of themselves (Matt. 7:21–22)
       a. Eyes closed to the emptiness of his own profession
       b. A form of godliness that doesn't change the life
  B. *Because of the Longsuffering of the Lord (v. 29)*
    1. The startled servants: Did not you sow good seed?
       a. Indicates real surprise and perplexity
       b. Didn't so-and-so come to know the Lord?
    2. The enthusiastic desire for church purity
    3. The tender and careful husbandman and the wheat
    4. God is longsuffering to us
  C. *Because the Day of Harvest Has Not Yet Arrived (v. 30)*
    1. The truth that evil will not be overcome until God intervenes

    2. Hypocrites get by and perhaps prosper until harvest
    3. What is meant by harvest (Rev. 14:14–20; 19:11–20)
       a. Looks on past the rapture, the tribulation, Armageddon
       b. The end of the age and the Father's kingdom
    4. Notice the tares in the harvest
       a. The appearance of good makes no eternal difference
       b. Association with good makes no difference
       c. Weeping and gnashing of teeth

III. Conclusion
    A. *What Does Hypocrisy in the Church Indicate?*
       1. Indicates the truth of the Bible
       2. Indicates the harvest
    B. *What Ought We to Do?*
       1. Examine ourselves to see if we are in the faith
       2. Study the gospel and seek its application
       3. Dispel darkness by the Word of God

Prepared Hearts

2 Chronicles 20:33

I. Introduction
   A. The Introduction to a King (Jehoshaphat)
1. The refreshing statement: he did that which was right (v. 32)
2. The revival under Jehoshaphat
    a. Teaching the people the Word of God
    b. Destroying of idolatry and images

   B. The Battle That Was Won with a Song
   C. The Contrast Between the King and His People
1. The King's heart prepared before the Lord (2 Chron. 19:3)
2. The people with unprepared hearts (2 Chron. 20:33)

II. Body
   A. Prepared Hearts Are Sensitive Hearts (2 Chron. 19:9)
1. Notice the king's care in instruction
2. Fear of the Lord
3. The age of hard hearts in mothers, fathers, and children
4. The almost absent tear
5. The strongest Man and the shortest verse (John 11:35)
6. Familiarity (Heb. 3:13; Mark 6:4, 52)

   B. Prepared Hearts Are Seeking Hearts (2 Chron. 20:3)
1. Jehoshaphat's prayer: he set himself to seek the Lord
2. Seeking to find peace with God
3. Seeking to experience God's power in battle
4. Seeking a closer walk with God (Phil. 3:13)
5. Seeking to hear a message from the Lord (Luke 24:5)

   C. Prepared Hearts Are Surrendered Hearts (2 Chron. 20)
1. The strange formula for the battle (v. 21)
2. Full surrender brings a spirit of praise (v. 21)
3. Full surrender brings victory (v. 24)
4. Full surrender brings rich reward (v. 25)
5. Full surrender brings joy and rejoicing (v. 27)

6. Full surrender affects others (v. 29)

III. Conclusion
- A. *Has God Been Preparing Your Heart?*
  1. Result of sin: familiarity and carelessness
  2. Through circumstances
- B. *Seek After Him and Surrender to His Will*
  1. Application to the unsaved
  2. Application to the Christian

Trouble Ahead

Job 38:22–23

I. Introduction
    A. *Introduction to Job*
        1. The oldest book? The righteous man
        2. Prospering in family, money, and property
    B. *Job and His Time of Trouble*
        1. Job's property taken; his family gone
        2. Job's health taken; words from his wife
    C. *God and His Word to Job in the Ash Pit*

II. Body
    A. *The Finite Holds No Standard to Guide Your Life*
        1. By *finite*, we mean all that has to do with man's wisdom. Man is finite; God is infinite
        2. The scene is the response of God to the end of man's figuring about Job's troubles
        3. Job's friends and their comfort (Job 2:11–12)
            a. Job 4:8–9; 5:17; 8:1–4; 11:3; 12:1–12
            b. High-sounding but false solutions
        4. Philosophic instruction, even on the nature of God, will be wrong unless based on God's Word entirely
        5. Danger in preaching on the words of Job's friends
        6. In contrast: God the Infinite One
    B. *The Future Holds No Secrets from God*
        1. The oldest book predicts the future
        2. More scientific hints than all uninspired literature
        3. The uncertainties of the future
            a. Your life or death date
            b. The future of governments
        4. Thrilling prophecy here: the hail; the time of trouble (Rev. 16:21)
    C. *The Fortunes of Earth Hold No Security to Guarantee Blessing*
        1. How much do you own? What shall it profit a man . . . ?
        2. How much in the bank? Could close tomorrow
        3. How strong do you feel? Dreaded disease could deteriorate your body even now

    4. What do you see about you? It is all to come crashing down

    5. Tribulation, war, and destruction

III. Conclusion

  A. *What Then Can Man Do?*

    1. Get to know the God who knows the future

    2. Job 42:1–5: faith springs up as never before

    3. No secondhand religion will satisfy in trouble

  B. *Get to Know God Today Through Christ*

The Right Hand of God

Ephesians 1:17–23

I. **Introduction**
    A. *The Neglected Ministry*
        1. The birth, the death, and the resurrection
        2. The resurrected, living Lord
    B. *The Scene at the Ascension*
        1. The disciples' desire for the kingdom
        2. The Comforter to come
        3. The heavenly scene
    C. *The Right Hand of the Father*

II. **Body**
    A. *The Place of Authority (vv. 20–23)*
        1. The great contrast to earthly experience
        2. Men spit upon Him, but angels sing His praises
        3. Men persecuted Him, but heaven praises Him
        4. Earth rejected Him, but heaven rejoices over Him
        5. The Savior in authority and us
            a. The course of this world
            b. We're on the winning side
    B. *The Place of Accomplishment (Heb. 10:12)*
        1. The work on the cross completed: "It is finished"
        2. Sin is defeated: Jesus tempted in all points but without sin
        3. Satan defeated: Jesus came to destroy works of the Devil
        4. Death defeated (1 Cor. 15:51)
        5. The firstfruits of heaven (1 Cor. 15:20–23)
        6. The sinner in heavenly places (Eph. 2:6–9)
    C. *The Place of the Advocate (1 John 2:1)*
        1. How I need an advocate like Him
        2. Peter: we are kept by the power of God
        3. Paul: we are saved by His life (Rom. 5:10)
        4. The Perfect Mediator, superior to the saints (Acts 7:55–56)

III. **Conclusion**
    A. *The Application to the Sinner*

    1. Salvation accomplished for you
    2. A living Savior to keep you
  B. *The Application to the Saint*
    1. For the wanderer: come to your advocate
    2. For the troubled one: rest in His work for you

She Hath Done What She Could!

Mark 14:8

I. **Introduction**
 A. *Difficult Days for the Savior*
  1. They plotted to put Him to death (Mark 14:1)
  2. Critics and enemies were all about Him
 B. *The Meal in the House of Simon the Leper (Mark 14:3)*
  1. The woman with the box of precious ointment
  2. The reaction of the people present
  3. The response of Jesus

II. **Body**
 A. *She Did What She Could with What She Had*
  1. Some think of what they would do
  2. Some gripe about what others don't do
  3. She did what she could with what she had (Give examples of people who have done what they could with what they had—sending out letters and cards of encouragement, prayers, etc.)
 B. *She Did What She Could While She Could*
  1. Some are always going to do something sometime
  2. Some are great "tomorrow people"
  3. Some believe in yesterday
  4. Some are always waiting for the right moment
 C. *She Did What She Could Regardless of the Critics*
  1. There will always be complainers
  2. Some specialize in faultfinding
 D. *She Did What She Could for Jesus*
  1. Her motive was right
  2. What is your motive for Christian service?
  3. Rewards come for right motives

III. **Conclusion**
 A. *A Great Statement for Life: "She Hath Done What She Could"*
 B. *What Will You Do with What You Have?*

The Judgment of God

I. Introduction
  A. *The Reality of Sin*
  1. An introduction for preaching on Romans 3
  2. God seeks to make us aware of our greatest problem
     a. Through disease
     b. Through poverty
     c. Through destruction
  3. Our safety efforts and salvation efforts
  B. *The Effects of Sin*
  1. Socially and spiritually (Rom. 1)
  2. The coming judgment in view (Rom. 2:5–16)
  3. Not only consequences here but hereafter (Rev. 20)

III. Body
  A. *The Judgment of God Is According to Truth (v. 2)*
  1. Perhaps the hardest thing to apply when judging
  2. When judging loved ones, we are often partial
     a. We allow our hearts to rule our heads
     b. We bend truth because of who is involved
  3. When judging ourselves we are often blind (v. 1)
     a. Ephesians 5:29: "no man ever yet hated his own flesh"
     b. Pride distorts the picture
  B. *The Judgment of God Is According to Accumulated Wrath (v. 5)*
  1. The privilege of laying up treasures in heaven
  2. The frightening thought of treasuring up wrath
     a. By despising the riches of God's goodness
     b. By rejecting the pleas of God to come to repentance
  3. Cannot get away with constant rejections
     a. Consider Jerusalem
     b. Consider Felix
  C. *The Judgment of God Is According to Works (v. 6)*
  1. Not salvation by works (Eph. 2:8–9)
  2. God is just, right up to the minutest detail

        a. Rev. 20:12: according to works
        b. Luke 10:13–14: tolerable for Tyre and Sidon
    3. Degrees of punishment, not duration of punishment
    4. Don't misunderstand; no one saved but through Christ
  D. *The Judgment of God Is According to Complete Impartiality*
    1. What a problem is this daily practice
    2. James 2:1–6: the problem in the church
    3. If you know the right person
    4. If you hold the right title
  E. *The Judgment of God Is According to All the Facts (v. 16)*
    1. God shall judge the secrets of men
    2. Man's heart is wicked
        a. Crime at night
        b. Secrets of thought and intent; covetousness

III. Conclusion
  A. *Summary and Application*
  B. *How to Escape the Final Judgment of God (John 5:24; Rom. 8:1)*

Getting Acquainted with Paul's Friend Onesiphorus

2 Timothy 1:16–18

I. Introduction
    A. *Meeting Onesiphorus*
        1. A believer from Ephesus
        2. He had been faithful to the work there
        3. When he came to Rome, he looked up Paul; may have been on a business trip
    B. *Onesiphorus—Dead or Alive?*
        1. "The Lord give mercy unto the house of . . ."
            a. A message to his family and for them
            b. Some think this means he had died
            c. See also 2 Timothy 4:19
        2. Was he dead or imprisoned?
            a. Did he die of natural causes?
            b. Did he die in a storm at sea returning home?
            c. Was he awaiting sentence because he dared identify with Paul?

II. Body
    A. *He Went Out of His Way to Visit Paul (v. 17)*
        1. The order of events is best seen by noting this first
        2. "He sought me out very diligently, and found me"
        3. Why was it hard to find Paul?
            a. Perhaps moved to various places in the prison
            b. Perhaps other Christians had feared to give out this information
        4. Going out of our way to reach others
        5. Going out of our way to minister to troubled believers
    B. *He Visited Paul Several Times (v. 16)*
        1. "He oft refreshed me"
        2. His interest in Paul was more than passing—not just duty
        3. He refreshed Paul
            a. Perhaps physically
            b. Perhaps socially—news from Ephesus about

            Timothy and others and the progress of the
work

    c. Perhaps spiritually—maybe even praying for
him and with him, discussing the Scriptures
and other books

  4. See Matthew 25:34–40

C. *He Was Not Ashamed of Paul's Chain (v. 16)*

  1. Not ashamed to be identified with Paul

    a. Onesiphorus was not ashamed to be a Christian

    b. Onesiphorus was not ashamed to be there with
Paul in prison

  2. Paul called his chains "the bonds of Christ"

  3. There are many kinds of chains

  4. A person's chains may lessen his circle of friends

    a. The chain of poverty

    b. The chain of unpopularity

    c. The chain of past sins

    d. The chain of past failures

III. Conclusion

A. *What a Friend!*

B. *May God Make Us Friends Who Minister to Others!*

The Armor of God

Ephesians 6:10–18

I. **Introduction**
  A. *The Command to Stand*
    1. Stand against the wiles of the Devil
    2. Stand fast in the faith
    3. Stand fast in one spirit and mind
  B. *But We Cannot Stand in Our Own Strength*
    1. The foe is too fierce and strong
    2. Therefore we are furnished with armor for defense

II. **Body**
  A. *The Belt of Truth*
    1. Clothing then: long, flowing robes for both men and women
      a. Beautiful, but clumsy when on the move
      b. Easy to get tangled when moving quickly
      c. Difficult for travel and terrible in battle
    2. The belt, or sash, held in their robes
      a. Israelites on the first Passover night (Exod. 12:11)
      b. Elijah girded up his loins to run before Ahab in the rain (1 Kings 18:46)
      c. The military sash: leather and metal, protected the lower part of the body
    3. The belt of truth
      a. Dishonesty is entangling
      b. Paul calls for total honesty
        (1) With ourselves
        (2) With others
    4. The opposite of hypocrisy
  B. *The Breastplate of Righteousness (v. 14)*
    1. Paul observing the Roman armor when a soldier walked by
      a. Breastplate: a coat of mail that protected the body from the neck to the hips
      b. Earliest were of tough skins; later, metal
    2. The breastplate protected the heart
    3. First mention in the Bible was the breastplate worn

by the high priest on the Day of Atonement
4. The prophecy of Jesus in Isaiah 59:17
5. Two kinds of righteousness
    a. Imputed: the result of faith (2 Cor. 5:21)
    b. Practical: do right, good works
6. Because it is right

C. *The Preparation of the Gospel of Peace (v. 15)*
    1. Roman soldiers and their shoes
    2. Shoes speak of being established, grounded
    3. Shoes speak of being on the move, progressing
    4. Preparation of the gospel of peace
        a. Understanding the basics of the gospel
        b. The gospel of peace for many troubled hearts
    5. Preparation, outreach, visitation, on the move

D. *The Shield of Faith (v. 16)*
    1. Above all, the shield of faith
    2. The words "above all" can mean "over all"
        a. Covering all areas—two kinds of shields
        b. Fully armed and protected
    3. Total trust quenches the fiery darts of the wicked
        a. The darts of pride, fear, lust, anxiety
        b. Faith wards off all arrows

E. *The Helmet of Salvation (v. 17)*
    1. This speaks of assurance of salvation
    2. I know whom I have believed
    3. D. L. Moody said he never knew anyone effective
       in serving Christ who did not have assurance of
       salvation
    4. If you don't know you're saved, get that settled
       today

F. *The Sword of the Spirit (v. 17)*
    1. The Word of God: the only offensive weapon
    2. Only one weapon for the Christian
        a. This weapon is the Bible
        b. Its mastery is needed to be a winner
    3. Consider Jesus in the temptation
    4. How about a new dedication to God's Word?

III. Conclusion
A. *Praying Always*
    1. The Christian's breath is absolutely vital

2. Communication with the Captain
B. *The Invincible Christian*
   1. Stands against any attack
   2. Put on the whole armor of God

Moses: Faith in Action

I. **Introduction**
   A. *The Chapter of Faith*
      1. God's march of mighty men and women
      2. Faith is the assurance of things hoped for—the conviction of their reality
   B. *Moses: Most Like Us in His Struggles*
      1. Not many called upon to build an ark (Noah)
      2. Won't have to hide spies on your roof (Rahab)
      3. God not starting a nation with you (Abraham)
      4. But the choices made by Moses are real to all of us

II. **Body**
   A. *What Moses' Faith Caused Him to Refuse*
      1. The faith of his parents (v. 23)
      2. Moses' faith: "When he was come to years"
         a. The faithful witness of Moses' mother
         b. Moses arrives at a commitment himself
            (1) "When he was come to years" similar to "When Peter was come to himself" (Acts 12:11)
            (2) We cannot depend on the faith of our parents
      3. This decision made him refuse a position
         a. He refused to be called the son of Pharoah's daughter
         b. Rank, power, honor, title
         c. Things that people work a lifetime to achieve; status
      4. This decision made him refuse certain pleasures
         a. Little that Moses could not have had there in Egypt
         b. The philosophy to live for the moment
      5. This decision made him refuse certain treasures
         a. The mighty treasures of Egypt
         b. What some men live for
   B. *What Moses' Faith Made Him Choose*
      1. He chose to be identified with a despised people

        a. The Israelites: rightful position, Joseph, Goshen
        b. Now they are slaves: despised, looked down
           upon
        c. Some do not come to Christ because they don't
           want to be identified as Christians
        d. You may even feel strange attending here today
    2. He chose the reproach of Christ
        a. What a strange statement about someone who
           lived 1,500 years before Christ
        b. But they were looking forward to His coming
        c. Moses identified himself with the coming
           Messiah
    3. Many flee from that reproach today
        a. How loosely they use His name in profanity
        b. He died publicly for you on the cross, and will
           you not walk down that aisle, go into the waters
           of baptism, witness, etc.?
    4. Moses' faith made him choose
  C. *What Moses' Faith Made Him See*
    1. He saw a reward beyond this life
        a. He had respect to the recompense of reward
        b. What shall it profit a man?
        c. How right he was! Egypt later in ruins; Moses'
           name lives on
    2. He saw the Lord (v. 27)
        a. Seeing Him who is invisible
        b. Peter: "Whom having not seen, ye love"
           (1 Peter 1:8)
        c. Moses is going to need that presence in the
           future
        d. The Invisible One carried him through

III. Conclusion
  A. *Have You "Come to Years"?*
  B. *What Has Your Faith Made You Refuse and Choose?*

Things Have Just Begun

I. **Introduction**
  A. *The Book of Philippians*
    1. A book of peace (Phil. 4:7)
    2. Christ provides strength (Phil. 4:13)
    3. Looking forward; looking upward (contrast: Phil. 2:4 with 2:21)
  B. *Introduction to the Book*
    1. Written about ten years after Paul's first visit
    2. From a prison cell with the shadow of death hanging over him
    3. Philippi: chief city of Macedonia, named after King Philip, father of Alexander the Great
    4. Fertile soil, gold and silver mines, on the route to Asia

II. **Body**
  A. *God Has Begun a Work (v. 6)*
    1. Paul's mind goes back to those first days
    2. The events in Acts 16
      a. The call in the night in Troas
      b. The conversion of Lydia: good, religious but lost, her family
      c. The fortune-teller's demon cast out
      d. The Philippian jailor, his family, their baptism
    3. Yes, God had begun a good work—at Calvary—in conversions
  B. *God Is Performing a Work Today (v. 6)*
    1. While Paul was in jail
    2. Even if Paul should lose his life
    3. God at work today
  C. *God Will Perform His Work to Completion (v. 6)*
    1. The definiteness of God's work: confident
    2. The degree of God's work: good
    3. The duration of God's work: until the day of Jesus
    4. The day of Jesus Christ: the day of rewards

III. **Conclusion**
  A. *The Outlook of Paul*
    1. The backward look (v. 3)
    2. The present look (vv. 4–5)
    3. The upward look
  B. *Things Have Just Begin! May God Grant It. Amen!*

The Wages of Sin

Romans 6:23

I. Introduction

A. *Most Used Road Signs*
1. The wages of sin is death
2. Prepare to meet thy God

B. *The Verse of Contrast*
1. Death and eternal life
2. Sin and the sinless one
3. Wages and gifts

II. Body

A. *The Wages of Sin*
1. "The wages of sin is death"
   a. Sin hastens physical death
   b. Sin holds one in spiritual death
   c. Sin's outcome is the second death
2. The topic of universal interest
   a. Wages, contracts, demands, hikes, deductions
   b. Minimum wage laws; wages and cost of living
3. The term "wages" indicates service for someone or something
   a. Romans 6:16: serving sin and Satan
   b. What a hideous employer
4. Sin and wages indicate work, drudgery, burdensome tasks
   a. Sin the work, Satan the employer: poverty of soul, no future, despondency
   b. The world usually thinks of sin as freedom
   c. The way of transgressors is hard (Prov. 13:15)
5. Death
   a. Spiritual death (Gen. 2:17)
   b. Physical death (Rom. 5:12)
   c. Second death (Rev. 20:12–15): separation

B. *The Wonderful Gift*
1. "The gift of God is eternal life"
2. The contrast of God's choosing brought into a dark picture
3. The usual presentation to the sinner at this point

4. God is the great giver (one of the most used words)
    a. Gave life to begin with; gave wife to Adam
    b. Rain, sunshine, and the beauties of nature
    c. Matt.11:28; John 1:12; 3:16
    d. Annie Johnson Flint's song, "He Giveth More Grace"
5. The gift of eternal life
    a. Puts to the lie all systems of works for salvation
    b. Ephesians 2:8–9: not of works but God's gift
    c. Joined eternally to God (1 John 5:11)
6. Eternal: begins when you get it and can never end
C. *The Way to Receive the Gift of God*
    1. "Through Jesus Christ our Lord"
    2. 1 John 5:11–13: This life is in His Son

III. Conclusion
A. *The Contrast in Closing*
B. *Take Christ; Take Life*

Some Things to Remember

Isaiah 6

I. Introduction
A. *Looking Back*
1. Satisfying to see good attendance
2. Satisfying to think of souls saved
3. Satisfying to see the number of people now serving the Lord

B. *Forgetting Those Things Which Are Behind*
1. Having looked at the past, let us praise God and go on
2. Whatever God has done is all to His glory

C. *Some Things to Remember*

II. Body
A. *Remember the Holy Character of Our God (vv. 1–4)*
1. In the year that King Uzziah died
   a. Uzziah was a great and powerful king
   b. When Uzziah died, Isaiah saw the Lord
2. What is God like?
   a. To some He is just a supreme being out there
   b. To some He is like an indulgent grandfather
   c. To some He is a force that started things and then left
3. But Isaiah found Him to be the thrice holy God
   a. Holy, Holy, Holy Trinity
   b. The sin in the garden could not be excused
   c. The people of Noah's day could not be allowed to live
   d. The cities of Sodom and Gomorrah could not stand
   e. Moses had to take off his shoes when before the bush
   f. Sinai and the borders to protect the people
4. Calvary's cross: the place where holiness and love met

B. *Remember to Keep a Tender Christian Conscience (v. 5)*
1. "Then said I, Woe is me!"

2. When Isaiah saw himself measured by God's standard
   a. Abraham: I am but dust and ashes
   b. Job: I am vile
   c. Paul: I am less than the least of all saints
   d. Peter: Depart from me, for I am a sinful man
3. Paul said that in the last days men would have their consciences seared with a hot iron
   a. Old-fashioned morality vs. the new morality
   b. Old-fashioned honesty vs. whether it is profitable
   c. Sex is used to sell everything from suits to soda pop
4. But the Christian must keep a tender conscience
   a. When he hears the first curse word
   b. When she reads the first questionable line in a book
   c. When the first thought of lust lingers in his heart
   d. When the first word of gossip passes her lips
   e. When the first dishonest dollar lies in his hand
5. At the first cry of conscience, run to the place of confession and cleansing

C. *Remember to Listen for the Voice of God (v. 9)*

III. Conclusion
A. *He May Be Calling You to Serve Him in the Harvest*
B. *He Has Called Many from Our Midst; You May Be Next*

The Departing Disciple

Acts 13:13

I. Introduction

A. *Following in the Footsteps of the First Missionaries*
1. From Antioch to Cyprus: preaching in the synagogues
2. Most exciting missionary account: pioneer missions

B. *From Paphos to Perga in Pamphylia*
1. The rejoicing governor
2. The 170 miles to Perga: the preparation
3. The greatest problem to face in Perga

C. *The Departing Disciple: Rough Going Ahead*

II. Body

A. *The Christian Must Realize That There Are Mountains to Cross*
1. Mark and his first impulse to missionary service
2. What we know of Mark from Acts 12:12: son of a rich woman
3. H. A. Ironside: "That isn't always the best start in life—to be born with a silver spoon in your mouth!"
   a. The tragedy of modern youth
   b. The mistake: won't have to work as I have
4. Crossing mountains
   a. Moses: must face Pharaoh to free Israel
   b. David: must face Goliath to defend Israel
   c. Many mountains today: ridicule, financial stress, family forsaking, physical suffering

B. *The Christian Must Not Retreat from Crossing the Mountains of Life Lest He Harm His Service for Christ (Acts 15:37)*
1. Mark's next desire for missionary service
2. The world is retreating from its problems
   a. The person imbibing alchohol is in retreat
   b. The loud cursing mouth is evidence of retreat
   c. The unfaithful woman is evidence of retreat
   d. The liar is in retreat
   e. The young person who runs with the worldly crowd is in retreat

   f. The slave to entertainment is in retreat
  3. Biblical examples of retreat
   a. Israel desiring to return to Egypt
   b. Peter's denial at the trial of Jesus
  4. Problems are never really solved by retreating from them
  5. Great men facing problemsfge.g., Daniel and his friends
 C. *The Christian Must Refresh Himself by Looking to Jesus*
  1. The difference in the problem for the Christian and the world
  2. Second Corinthians 12:7–10: Paul finding strength for mountains
  3. What happened to Mark?
   a. Wrote his gospel between these years
   b. Saw Christ facing and overcoming (Mark 1:12–13; 4:35–41; 14:22–46; 15:15–28)
  4. The profitable servant by looking to Jesus

III. Conclusion
 A. *What to Do with Mountains*
  1. Face them: conquer them with Christ
  2. Don't run from your problems today
 B. *Who Has Problems to Face?*

Peter Delivered from Prison

Acts 12

I. Introduction
   A. *Peter, James, and John*
   1. These three linked eternally with Jesus
   2. The intimate experiences
      a. The Mount of Transfiguration
      b. The house of Jairus
      c. The garden of Gethsemane
   B. *James Slain and Peter Captured*
   1. The people pleased; Herod popular; the politicians
   2. Peter faces death
   3. The church prays and Peter is saved
   C. *The Parable of Peter's Peril and the Answer to the Prayer of the Church*

II. Body
   A. *Peter in Prison (vv. 5–6)*
   1. The unconverted man is asleep
      a. He is asleep to the dangers ahead of him
      b. He is often asleep to the chains that hold him
      c. He is unconcerned about the judgment awaiting him
   2. The unconverted man is in the hands of the Enemy
      a. God has a great work for Peter to do, but Peter is chained
      b. God has a high calling for every man; are you chained?
      c. The unsaved man can never realize what God has for him while he is in Satan's power
   3. The unconverted man is chained in sin
      a. The chain of self
      b. The chain of Satan
   B. *The Praying Church (v. 5)*
   1. It is to any church's credit to be a praying church
   2. The church and the home that prays together stays together
   3. Not enough money to pay the bills, build the building, mow the lawn

a. The church that would move its area for God must pray
b. Members who would serve God must pray
c. It is impossible to build a great soul-winning church apart from much prayer
4. In our day a delegation might have been sent to influence Herod and resolutions might have been passed—but the early church prayed
5. Notice the result of their prayers
a. The angel of the Lord—the Holy Spirit—came upon Peter
b. The light shone in the prison: the Word of God
c. The angel struck him: wake up
d. The messenger of God spoke to him
e. The chains fell off

C. *Peter Delivered (vv. 7–11)*
1. Bind on thy sandals: walk like a free man
2. Follow me: follow God's instruction
3. Peter thought it was too good to be true
4. He passed the gate; tomorrow would have meant death
5. Assurance: "Now I know of a surety"
6. Searching out a praying church

III. Conclusion
A. *Surprising the Saints*
B. *The Church That Prays Is in for Some Miraculous Surprises*

October

The Church in Action

Acts 3:1–11

I. **Introduction**
   A. *The Association of Christ with the Suffering of the World*
      1. Not strange to find His disciples also interested
      2. The woman bound for thirty-eight years; blind Bartimaeus; the palsied man
   B. *The Pattern of New Testament Practice*
      1. Prayer
      2. Preaching
      3. Practice
   C. *The Setting and the Scene*
      1. The hour of prayer, 3:00 p.m.
      2. The unneeded sacrificed in the temple that day
      3. The spiritual application of the scene at the temple

II. **Body**
   A. *The Beggar in Want (vv. 1–3)*
      1. Lame from his mother's womb (Ps. 58:1–3; Rom. 3:23)
      2. Speculation as to duration of his illness
      3. Carried by others to the gate of the temple
      4. Many living on the world's handouts
      5. The mistaken idea of his need
      6. The beggar's request and response
   B. *The Servants of God at Work (vv. 4–7)*
      1. The look of compassion and not of scorn
      2. Peter's invitation: "Look on us"
      3. Our responsibility to have compassion on all men
      4. Silver and gold have I none but such as I have give I thee: Is this your testimony?
   C. *The World in Wonder (vv. 8–11)*
      1. From lame to leaping
      2. From sad to singing; from alms to hallelujahs
      3. The world cannot help but notice (v. 9)
      4. If any man be in Christ, he is a new creature
      5. The new walk of faith

III. **Conclusion**
   A. *Peter Taking Advantage of the Opportunity (vv. 12–26)*
   B. *Application and Call*

Afraid of What?

1 Peter 5:7

I. Introduction
    A. A Great Verse for Troubled People
1. You are in this verse
2. Your cares are in this verse
3. Jesus is in this verse

    B. But What Are the Cares That Trouble People?
    C. What Makes People Afraid to Face Life?

II. Body
    A. Fears Concerning Those We Love
1. The loving parent's priority: their children
   a. Checking babies in the night
   b. Fevered and fractured children
   c. Waiting outside intensive care units
2. Fears about husbands and wives
   a. Perhaps you fear the loss of his or her love
   b. You worry about loss of jobs
   c. Concerns about the health of a mate
3. Bible examples
   a. The healing of Jairus's daughter
   b. Mary and Martha send for Jesus because of Lazarus
   c. Jesus' provision for his mother at the cross

    B. Fears Concerning Health
1. These bodies are sources of anxiety; they are fearfully and wonderfully made
2. The danger of hypochondria
3. To some, contamination is a constant fear
   a. Unusual feelings, danger signs
   b. Publicity concerning symptoms
   c. Pollution because of technology
   d. Exposure to Internet/media articles

    C. Fears Concerning Financial Security
1. The necessity of having money
2. The danger when money has us; love of money is the root of all kinds of evil

3. Two things never to worry about: weather and money
    a. You can't change the weather—and it will change
    b. Those with more money have more worries and depression
4. The uselessness of hoarding gold in the end times

D. *The Fear of People*
   1. The fear of man bringeth a snare (Prov. 29:25)
   2. Speaking before a crowd
      a. Moses identified with that (Exod. 4)
      b. Jeremiah's fear (Jer. 1)
   3. Fear of public exposure to people holds back many
   4. Jobs are out of reach because they necessitate meeting people
   5. Christian work is passed over because of fear of people

E. *The Fear of Failure and of Success*
   1. Unwilling to try anything new; fear of disappointment
   2. Not daring to invest, unwilling to marry—but there are unlimited horizons
   3. Whatsoever is not of faith is sin; much is lost because of such sin
   4. Some fear to succeed; unsure how to handle success

F. *The Fear of Death, Which Involves the Fear of Eternity*
   1. Some fears are legitimate
      a. Death comes to all (Heb. 9:27)
      b. All should prepare to meet God (Amos 4:12)
      c. Sensible survival practices should be a part of life
   2. Some expect destruction continually
      a. Live in constant fear of attack
      b. Fear of riding in cars, planes, boats, etc.
      c. Death seems to await at the end of every illness
   3. We can be saved and ready for death and eternity
   4. We do not have to be trembling about the hereafter
      a. Some continually fear the unpardonable sin
      b. Some fear they aren't really saved; get it settled
   5. For me to live is Christ and to die is gain

III. **Conclusion**
   A. *Cast Your Cares on Jesus*
   B. *Perfect Peace Can Be Yours*

Epitaph:

Here lies a man who lived to age
Yet still from death was flying;
Who, though not sick, was never well
And died from fear of dying.

From Death to Life

John 11:38–44

I. Introduction
   A. *The Wonderful Tenth Chapter of John*
      1. What a background for this Scripture
      2. The stoning incident and Jesus' departure for another place
      3. The success and revival there
   B. *The Call to Come to the Aid of Lazarus*
      1. Jesus responds in spite of danger
      2. The resurrection of Lazarus
   C. *A Picture of the Salvation of Any Sinner*
      1. Dead in sin; through salvation made spiritually alive
      2. See then the lesson for us

II. Body
   A. *The Responsibility of the Disciples in Bringing Life*
      1. Remove the stone
      2. Why not by His great power alone?
         a. He chooses to use His own
         b. The Great Commission was not to angels
      3. Gravestones are interesting things—sometimes humorous
         a. Stones with dates and poems
         b. Pictures of the deceased
      4. Symbolically, the stone stands for anything that stands between the lost person and Christ
         a. Temper
         b. Tongue
         c. Habits
         d. Hypocrisy
         e. Gossip
         f. Criticism
         g. Unbelief
   B. *The Resurrection Itself Was Entirely by the Power of God*
      1. The great miracle
         a. Dead for four days

161

       b. An impossible accomplishment
2. The dead in sin made alive by the power of Christ
    a. Rom. 5:12–17
    b. 1 Cor. 15:20–22
3. We cannot save anyone ourselves
4. Give out the Word and trust the Holy Spirit to do the saving

C. *The Release of Lazarus Was Done by the Disciples*
1. Alive but bound
2. Showing signs of life, but still carries the appearance of the grave
3. Graveclothes now need to be removed
    a. Face: eyes behold the beauty of the Lord
    b. Mouth to speak for the Lord
    c. Arms to work for the Lord
    d. Feet to go for the Lord

III. Conclusion
A. *The Rejoicing*
B. *The Deliverance of Souls*

From Tears to Triumph

Psalm 84

I. **Introduction**
   A. *The Psalms Are Personal*
      1. Depicting the many moods of life
      2. Joy, despair, triumph, tears, sin, forgiveness, worship
   B. *The Source of Blessing*
      1. God's blesses man
      2. Today—more about blessing
      3. Does anyone here not want God's blessing?

II. **Body**
   A. *Blessed Are They Who Dwell in Thy House*
      1. The Old Testament: God manifests Himself in the temple
         a. Here the animal sacrifices are made
         b. Here God will teach many lessons about Christ
         c. God makes His presence known (2 Chron. 7)
      2. The longing of the psalmist to be there at the temple
         a. "My soul longeth" (v. 2)
         b. His envy of the sparrows who can stay there
      3. In a very real sense, this is true in the gathering of God's people
         a. Anyone who has once loved the gathering with God's people especially misses it when he can no longer be there
         b. How many now on beds of affliction would like to be here
      4. But there is a greater truth
         a. Jesus begins to teach it in John 14:16–23
         b. On the day of Pentecost this begins
         c. Paul makes this teaching clearer (1 Cor. 6:19–20)
      5. So—blessed is the man who is in constant communion with Christ

B. *Blessed Is the Man Whose Strength Is in Thee (v. 5)*
   1. This indwelling presence of God becomes a source of strength
      a. Not only peace but power
      b. Not only feeling but fuel
   2. How many times our human strength fails
      a. Just when we think we have it all pumped up, the Devil pokes a nail through our balloon
      b. God lets us see just how weak we are without Him
   3. Spiritual weakness is the greatest weakness of all
      a. Makes us open to temptation to sin
      b. Makes us open to temptation to doubt, pout, grumble, grudge
   4. Strength is available from the Lord
      a. Pss. 27:14; 37:39
      b. Isa. 40; Phil. 4:13
   5. What this strength of God can do
      a. Reaches even to the valley of Baca (v. 6)
      b. Changes tears to triumph
C. *Blessed Is the Man That Trusteth in Thee (v. 12)*
   1. Not a new part of the formula but a summation
   2. No one can know His presence without trusting in Him
   3. No one can have His strength without first trusting in Him
   4. But note the many blessings to the man who trusts in Him
      a. The direction of the Lord (Prov. 3:5–6)
      b. Peace of mind (Isa. 26:3)
      c. Shall not be left alone (Ps. 34:22)
   5. "Trust in the Lord": Old Testament phrase used 152 times. Believe on the Lord Jesus Christ

III. Conclusion
A. *You Must Start with Trusting Before You Can Triumph*
B. *Application*

Lift Up Your Eyes

Psalm 121:1; John 4:35; Luke 21:28

I. Introduction
- A. *Four Life-Changing Words: Lift Up Your Eyes*
  1. Words of hope
  2. Words of challenge
- B. *Lift Up Your Eyes Above Man—So Many Fall Because of Looking at Man*

II. Body
- A. *We Need to Lift Up Our Eyes for Help (Ps. 121:1)*
  1. So many things are beyond our control
  2. There is a limit to our human ability
  3. The church is in need of help
     - a. We must be guided safely through the days ahead
     - b. Christian love must be our daily experience
     - c. We cannot afford the luxury of division
     - d. We must find and do the will of God
  4. We are in need of help as individuals
  5. It is through prayer that we enlist God's help
- B. *We Need to Lift Up Our Eyes to the Harvest (John 4:35)*
  1. The greatest area of defeat in the Christian life
  2. Soul winning keeps the church right with the Lord and others
  3. If the harvest was white in the day of Christ, how much more now?
  4. Ought to send Christians out to visit the lost
  5. Ought to make us concerned for all we meet
  6. Ought to raise up those for the foreign field
- C. *We Need to Lift Up Our Eyes for His Coming (Luke 21:28)*
  1. The present condition on earth
  2. Consider many signs now in the world for His return
  3. Your redemption draweth nigh
     - a. Not the end of the world
     - b. The return of the Lord for His people
     - c. Then we shall be what we should be

165

    4. The purifying hope
    5. Vance Havner: "We have no business living ordinary lives in such extraordinary times."

III. Conclusion
    A. *A Call to the Discouraged*
    B. *The Challenge of the Call*

Let's Get Excited About Soul Winning

Luke 15:10

I. Introduction
   A. *Let's Get Excited*
1. Let's get excited about Jesus
2. Let's get excited about the gospel
3. Let's get excited about salvation
4. Let's get excited about soul winning

   B. *Joy in the Presence of Angels of God*
1. Not only by angels, but in their presence
2. Christians in heaven made happy each time another is saved on earth
3. Why is soul winning so important?

II. Body
   A. *Because of the Importance of the Soul (Mark 8:36)*
1. The mad race to possess things
2. The title deed to the earth would not be enough to compensate for the loss of a soul
3. How much attention we give to the body
    a. Fitness, dressing up, fixing up
    b. The millions spent on health care
4. Compare this to the small amount spent on winning souls
5. Think how little time is spent or money invested by the average church in soul winning

   B. *Because of the Reality of Both Heaven and Hell*
1. Believers go to heaven when they die
    a. What a wonderful confidence this is!
    b. To be absent from the body is to be present with the Lord
    c. To die is gain
2. But it is equally true that lost people go to hell
    a. The forgotten teaching of our day
    b. Few sermons preached on hell anymore
3. Consider who cares if a sinner goes to hell (Luke 16)

   C. *Because of the Swift Passing of Time*
1. Today marks another landmark of time in our lives

2. It seems but a moment since we began the new year
3. How many opportunities were lost?
4. How many dropped from our ranks?
5. The importance of reaping at all ages
   D. *Because of the Soon Coming of Jesus*
      1. We are one year closer to the coming of Christ
      2. Signs of His coming multiply
      3. The time of our opportunity to witness is shrinking
      4. Jesus may come before this year has ended

III. Conclusion
   A. *Consider the Possibilities*
   B. *What May Happen if You Get Excited About Soul Winning*

Citizens of Heaven

I. Introduction
  A. *The Desire to See But Not to Settle*
   1. The freedoms we enjoy
   2. The privileges we enjoy
  B. *Citizens of the Perfect Land, Heaven*
  C. *Requirements of Citizens of Any Land*
   1. The new birth
   2. Entirely foreign to the natural mind

II. Body
  A. *There Is Cause to Rejoice (Phil. 3:1)*
   1. Paul, a Roman citizen, writing from a Roman prison
   2. This familiar characteristic to those in Philippi
   3. Jesus: rejoice because your names are written in heaven
   4. Perilous times in the world—rejoice
  B. *We Are to Be Pilgrims and Strangers in the World (1 Peter 2:11)*
   1. This world is not my home
   2. The man called a fool by Jesus—the only one
   3. Lay up your treasures in heaven
  C. *We Are to Realize Our Grave Responsibility (v. 10)*
   1. American citizens in a foreign land
   2. Other lands have wrong impression of us
   3. Let us represent heaven rightly
  D. *We Are to Anticipate Our Gracious Reward (vv. 20–21)*
   1. The Lord's responsibility to His own
   2. The power that will change our bodies
   3. What heaven is like

III. Conclusion
  A. *Why This Citizenship Is Available to Us*
  B. *Citizen of Heaven Became a Citizen of Earth—The Man Without a Country*

Naaman's Cleansing

2 Kings 5:1–14

I. Introduction
  A. *The Man with a Passion for Power*
  B. *Search the Scriptures—They Are They Which Testify of Me*
    1. The reason for recording such an account
    2. The beautiful gospel application here for us all
  C. *Naaman's Cleansing*

II. Body
  A. *Naaman and His Need (v. 1)*
    1. Ben-Hadad the king delegates responsibilities to Naaman
    2. Naaman: a great man in the sight of the king
    3. Honorable and honored, held in high esteem by the people
    4. His need: he was a leper
      a. His prominence, but a leper; his power, but a leper
      b. His last thought at night and the first in the morning
      c. The emptiness of all his accomplishments
    5. Leprosy as a type of sin, and the application of that to our lives
  B. *The Little Maid and Her Little Message (vv. 2–4)*
    1. The Syrians by companies, marauding bands—gurerilla type
    2. Slaves for the market and for the Syrians
    3. Another mother's day message: the little girl's faith
      a. Children under stress: Daniel, Moses, Joseph
      b. How will our children react? Have we prepared them?
    4. Note her concern, her compassion, and her confidence
    5. The pattern of simple faith in testifying that would move men for Christ
  C. *The Prophet and His Prescription (vv. 8–14)*
    1. Naaman to the king: king's letters and doctor's fee

2. The plight of the king of Israel and Elisha's message
3. Naaman at Elisha's door
   a. Naaman's pride: Elisha deals with it
   b. Naaman's preconceived notions: Elisha deals with them
   c. Naaman's other way: the rivers of Damascus; the offense of the cross
   d. Naaman's anger: good sign
4. The urging of the servants; their words true today as well

III. Conclusion
   A. *The Leper Cleansed (v. 14)*
      1. Faith demonstrated and faith rewarded
      2. Simple solution but necessary
   B. *The Sinner Clean*
      1. Sin of the leprosy of the race
      2. Plunge in the fountain for cleansing

Communion—or a Communion Service

1 Corinthians 11:23–34

I. **Introduction**
  A. *We Could Have Just Another Communion Service*
   1. The first Communion with Jesus and His disciples
   2. Our Lord's instruction for this to continue
   3. A Communion service can become formalistic, a monthly ritual
  B. *Let's Have Communion*
   1. Definition of *communion*: a mutual sharing of thoughts, feelings: fellowship
   2. This dimension of *communion* is like many Bible experiences
     a. Adam and Eve and the Lord before the fall
     b. Mary sitting at the feet of Jesus listening
     c. Moses at the burning bush and on Mt. Sinai
     d. Jesus and "Emmaus disciples"
  C. *Why the Lord's Table Is Called Communion*

II. **Body**
  A. *At the Cross, Communion with God Begins (vv. 23–25)*
   1. The Lord's Table more than a meal: it is a message
     a. "This is my body"
     b. "This is my blood"
   2. The word of Isaiah and Zechariah to be fulfilled
     a. He was to be wounded for us all (Isa. 53:5)
     b. They would look upon the Pierced One (Zech. 12:10)
   3. All believers begin at the cross
  B. *The Lord's Coming: Communion Will Be Complete (v. 26)*
   1. Today, we walk by faith and not by sight
   2. Then, faith will be lost in sight
   3. Today, we look at these symbols and think of the cross
   4. Then, we will look at our Savior and think of His love
   5. Today, we take this bread in our hands
   6. Then, we will take the hand of the Bread of Life

      7. Today, we share this fruit of the vine

      8. Then, we will share with the True Vine

  C. *At Confession of Sin, Communion Continues (vv. 28–32)*

      1. We have considered the beginning and the hope of the Christian life

         a. You look back to a day of salvation with assurance

         b. You look forward to meeting Christ with great joy

      2. But what about the time in between—what about now?

         a. You find yourself defeated by the Tempter

         b. You have been overcome by some sin

         c. You are not living on the mountaintop

         d. Your devotional life is dull or nonexistent

         e. You are discouraged by your failures

      3. It is time now for self-examination, self-judgment

      4. Confession of sin restores communion (1 John 1:9)

III. Conclusion

  A. *What Will You Confess to Christ Before Partaking of Communion?*

  B. *What Will You Do to Make This a Real Time of Communion?*

The Rat Race

Ecclesiastes 2

I. **Introduction**
   A. *On a Graduation Card: "Welcome to the Rat Race!" —*
      The right expression to describe today's hurried
      pace
   B. *Why This Busy Pace in Our Day*
      1. To maintain this thing we call standard of living
      2. The search for meaning in life
   C. *The Man in a Rat Race Long Ago: Solomon*

II. **Body**
   A. *The Rat Race*
      1. The book in the Bible for contrast
         a. The key phrase: "under the sun"
         b. Life as seen by the natural man
      2. Solomon and his search
      3. Solomon searches in education and philosophy
         a. Searches out the reason for all things under the sun
         b. Observes the phenomena of nature
         c. Tries to understand why things happen as they do
         d. Finds frustration (Eccl. 1:14–15)
         e. The more he knows, the worse he feels (Eccl. 1:18)
      4. Solomon intensifies his search and tries pleasure and feelings
         a. He tries mirth but finds misery
         b. He tries comedy but finds chaos
         c. He tries wine but finds it wanting
         d. He tries diversion but finds it disappointing
      5. Solomon tries to find meaning in great projects
         a. He tries architecture and agriculture (vv. 4–6)
         b. He tries mansions and music (v. 8)
         c. He tries power and position (vv. 9–11)
      6. What shall it profit a man if he shall gain the whole world?
   B. *How to Know if You Are in the Rat Race*

174

1. If you are exhausting yourself to gain material possessions
2. If you work night and day to keep up with others
3. If you are just getting yourself high for the feeling of the moment
4. If your life centers around yourself instead of others
5. If you are building your life without the Lord (Ps. 127:1)
C. *How to Get Out of the Rat Race and Into the Right Race*
   1. First, come with your sins to Christ
   2. Second, look to Him alone for your salvation
   3. Third, lay aside every weight and every sin
   4. Fourth, you must run with patience, steadfastness, and consistency
   5. Fifth, keep your eyes on Jesus

III. Conclusion
A. *If You Give of Yourself in This Race, You Will Not Be Sorry at the End*
B. *Matthew 10:39: "He that findeth his life shall lose it: and he that loseth his life for my sake shall find it"*

The Parable of the Wheat and the Tares

Matthew 13:24–30, 36–43

I. Introduction
A. *The Parable of the Wheat and the Tares*
   1. The scene of the sower sowing his seed
   2. The scene of the tares growing up with the wheat
   3. The disturbed servants and their suggestion
B. *The Interpretation of the Parable*

II. Body
A. *The Lord and His Eternal Purpose (vv. 24 and 37–38)*
   1. He that soweth good seed is the Son of man (v. 37)
   2. The field is the world (v. 38)
   3. The good seed are the children of the kingdom (v. 38)
   4. The Lord's purpose and His use of men
      a. The cross—the disciples—the commission
      b. Even the persecution and its purpose (Acts 8)
      c. True of the plagues in Egypt (Exod. 12)
      d. True of Israel's preservation (Deut. 29:6)
B. *The Sinner and His Eternal Perdition (vv. 25–30)*
   1. The tares growing and their characteristics
      a. Just like the wheat in early stages
      b. Fruit bearing (Gal. 5:16–23)
   2. This is undoubtedly the religious hypocrite
   3. Matthew 25:31–46: "Depart from me ye cursed"
C. *The Christian and the Eternal Prize (vv. 26, 43)*
   1. One in whom the seed of the Word has lodged
   2. He is now a good seed—a living epistle
   3. The Christian's privilege to bring forth fruit
      a. Must die to the world and self (John 12:24)
      b. Must abide in Christ and He in you (John 15)
      c. He that saveth his life shall lose it

III. Conclusion
A. *The Savior's Typical Conclusion*
   1. The appeal to the individual
   2. Some will be lost; will it be you?

3. Some will be fruitful; will it be you?
4. Some will shine as the sun; will you?
B. *He Who Hath Ears to Hear, Let Him Hear*

Tears in the Eyes of God

Luke 19:41–44

I. **Introduction**
   A. *Recorded Occasions of Jesus Weeping*
      1. The tomb of Lazarus and its implications
      2. The scene near Jerusalem
   B. *The Setting and the Scene*
      1. The triumphal entry
      2. The day before His trial and crucifixion
   C. *Tears in the Eyes of God and Why*

II. **Body**
   A. *He Saw the Persistence of Jerusalem's Problems (v. 41)*
      1. He beheld the city and wept over it
      2. Christ able to see the needy hearts of men
         a. The weary who would find no rest without Him
         b. The troubled who would find no peace without Him
         c. The young men who would find no satisfaction without Him
         d. The old men who would go to the grave without Him
         e. The sinner who would find no cleansing without Him
      3. Christ beholds your particular need today and longs to meet it
      4. The birth in Bethlehem miles south, thirty-three years before
      5. The angels' song and the message of the angel to the shepherds
   B. *He Saw the Toppling of Jerusalem's Treasures (vv. 43–44)*
      1. Not one stone left upon another
      2. The tall and proud buildings
      3. The temple incident
      4. The rich as well as the poor to be reduced to nothing
      5. The parable of the foolish man: not one thing left

6. If you build your treasures here, they will also topple
C. *He Saw the Missing of Jerusalem's Greatest Moment (v. 44)*
    1. You did not recognize the time of your visitation
    2. Her great moments through the years
        a. The head of Goliath carried into Jerusalem
        b. The ark of God in Jerusalem in the temple
        c. The armies of David in Jerusalem; the temple of Solomon
        d. The rebuilding of Jerusalem under Ezra
    3. The feasts in Jerusalem
    4. The Passover going on at that time
    5. The greatest moments were when the Savior had walked her streets

III. **Conclusion**
    A. *Summary and Application*
        1. Problems persist without Christ
        2. Treasures are temporary without Christ
        3. The greatest moment is when Christ speaks
    B. *Your Greatest Moment Is This Moment*

The God of All Comfort

2 Corinthians 1:2–3

I. Introduction

A. *Consider Job and His Great Loss*
1. The father of ten children
2. A wealthy and healthy man
3. Suddenly, tragedy—everything gone!

B. *Job's Secret: He Trusted the Lord*
1. In all this Job did not charge God foolishly
2. "The Lord gave and the Lord hath taken away"
3. "I know that my Redeemer liveth"

C. *Who Is This God Whom Job Trusted?*

II. Body

A. *He Is the Father of Our Lord Jesus Christ (v.3)*
1. The very fact that He sent His Son shows His love
2. Think how this shows His understanding
   a. Jesus endured great persecution
   b. Jesus endured the awful trial and scourging
   c. Jesus endured the cross and death
3. Do you wonder if God knows how you feel?
   a. Wonder no longer!
   b. Stand at the cross as He gives His Son
4. God understands your heartache

B. *He Is the Father of Mercies (v. 3)*
1. In the loss of a child, sometimes we question God's mercy
   a. Where was God when my child died?
   b. Why didn't God heal my child?
2. We do not know the answers now
   a. He will let us know in heaven
   b. We question because we do not know the whole picture
3. But we do know that He is the God of mercy
4. Someday we will know that every act of God is merciful

C. *He Is the God of All Comfort (v. 3)*
1. Paul needed comfort often
2. We need comfort in many circumstances

3. We may especially need comfort today
4. God, who understands, will give comfort
5. The Spirit of God is called "the Comforter"

III. Conclusion
   A. *Application of God's Comfort in Your Life*
   B. *Comfort One Another*

It Will Pay to Obey—Start Today

1 Samuel 15:22

I. Introduction
    A. Children and Obedience
        1. The importance of obedience in the home
        2. The present reaping of parents' laxness in this
    B. The Setting and the Scene of This Scripture
        1. Saul commanded to destroy the Amalekites
        2. His feeble explanation to Samuel
        3. To obey is greater than sacrifice
    C. How Can I Obey God?

II. Body
    A. You Can Obey God by Coming in Faith to Jesus Christ (1 John 3:23)
        1. The word *believe* means to trust
        2. This involved many calls to come to Jesus
            a. Matt. 11:28; John 7:37; Rev. 22:17
            b. The parable of the wedding feast (Matt. 22:1–14)
        3. This is the first step of obedience a man can take
        4. All but the human heart obeys Him—creation, the sea, the fig tree, the grave
    B. You Can Obey God by Confessing Jesus Christ Before Men (Matt. 10:32)
        1. You shall be witnesses unto me (Acts 1:8)
        2. Identified with Christ in heaven at salvation
        3. We are to be identified with Him here below
        4. Some like Joseph and Nicodemus are trying to be secret disciples
            a. You have never walked an aisle
            b. You have never been baptized
            c. You have never told anyone about your conversion
        5. If someone on earth does something, we want to let others know
    C. You Can Obey God by Conforming Your Life to the Teaching and Example of Jesus Christ (Luke 6:46)

1. So careful to teach that salvation is not by works
2. We must never forget that under God our lives are to be fashioned like Jesus
3. Christ the great example of obedience (Heb. 10:7)
4. Will you obey Him and His Word?
    a. Seek first the kingdom of God
    b. Lay up treasures in heaven
    c. Follow Me
    d. Be separate from the world
5. Antioch and "Christians"; what about you?

III. Conclusion
  A. *The Contrast Between Obedience and Disobedience*
    1. The two Sauls
    2. The ten lepers
  B. *What Will You Do?*

When a Christian Sins

Romans 6:1–2; Hebrews 12:6–8

I. **Introduction**
   A. *The Greatest Problem*
      1. Sin that made the cross necessary
      2. God's miraculous provision
      3. The sins of the past are all gone at last
   B. *The Security of the Believer*
      1. Rom. 8:38–39; Eph. 4:30; Heb. 7:25
      2. John 10:28–29; 1 John 5:13
   C. *The Two Great Errors*
      1. License on the part of the Christian
      2. Perceived looseness on the part of God; Isaiah 6—
         God's holiness

II. **Body**
   A. *Sin Will Affect Your Fellowship (1 John 1:7–9)*
      1. The sweet privilege of fellowship
         a. Adam and Eve in Eden
         b. Fellowship restored
      2. Walking in darkness destroys fellowship
         a. Works of darkness (Rom. 13:13; Eph. 5:1–8)
         b. Isa. 59:1–2; Ps. 66:18
   B. *Sin Will Affect Your Family (2 Sam. 12:1–14)*
      1. David's sin put away—but child dies
      2. Sin will affect by example
      3. The family sees the inconsistencies (e.g., Lot)
   C. *Sin Will Affect You Physically (1 Cor. 11:30)*
      1. The scene is the Communion service, but the issue
         is sin
      2. The case of Samson: from strong man to slave
      3. The case of mental anguish: think on these things
      4. The case of sins that affect the body
   D. *Sin Will Affect You Forever (1 Cor. 3)*
      1. At His coming: shame
      2. The case of the judgment seat
      3. He will suffer loss

III. **Conclusion**
  A. *What Shall the Christian Do?*
      1.   Judge yourself (1 Cor. 11:31)
      2.   Confess your sins (1 John 1:9)
      3.   Forsake (Prov. 28:13)
  B. *Where Shall the Sinner Appear? (1 Peter 4:17–18)*

When God Answers Prayer

Psalm 28:6–7

I. **Introduction**
   A. *Who Has Not Prayed in Times of Trouble?*
      1. Praying in crisis is as natural as breathing
      2. Praising God for answers is another matter
         a. After the storm, we often forget who rescued us
         b. When answers come, we may forget to give thanks
   B. *The Psalmist Raised His Voice in Grateful Praise*
      1. He is a good example to us all
      2. Consider his reasons for thankfulness

II. **Body**
   A. *God Had Heard His Prayers (v. 6)*
      1. "He hath heard the voice of my supplications"
      2. See how personal David is in his praying
         a. "O LORD my rock; be not silent to me" (v. 1)
         b. David prays from a personal walk with God
         c. He sees God as his firm foundation
      3. David prays with fervent urgency
         a. He feels he will die unless God answers
         b. He lifts his hands toward the temple
         c. He pleads for answers that vindicate righteousness
      4. When answers arrive, he gives God glory: "Blessed be the LORD"
   B. *God Had Honored His Faith (v. 7)*
      1. "My heart trusted in Him, and I am helped"
      2. All of God's blessings flow from faith
         a. We are saved by faith (Rom. 5:1; Eph. 2:8–9)
         b. We are to live by faith (Rom. 1:17)
         c. We are to pray in faith (James 1:6)
      3. Faith brought David strength: "The LORD is my strength"
      4. Faith brought David protection: "my shield"
      5. God still honors faith, so why are we worrying?
      6. Let's stop trembling and start trusting

C. *God Had Helped Him (v. 7)*
  1. "I am helped"
     a. C. H. Spurgeon: "Every day the believer may say, 'I am helped.'"
     b. Isaiah's promise: "I will help thee" (Isa. 41:10, 13)
  2. What God's help did for David
     a. Caused him to rejoice
     b. Gave him a song
     c. Filled his heart with praise
  3. C. H. Spurgeon: "Those who pray well will soon praise well."

III. **Conclusion**
  A. *Have You Dared Pray with Fervent Urgency?*
  B. *Has God Answered Prayer for You?*
  C. *Have You Responded with Thanksgiving and Praise?*

Changed Men

1 Peter 4:1–10

I. Introduction
  A. *Peter and the Sufferings and Death of Christ*
   1. The precious blood of Jesus (1 Peter 1:18–19)
   2. Who his own self bare our sins (1 Peter 2:21–25)
   3. The just for the unjust (1 Peter 3:18)
  B. *No Wonder! Peter Was There!*
   1. From the first revelation, he had dreaded it
   2. When it was near, he resolved, "I will never forsake you"
   3. To make it worse, his denial, his tears, and the cross
  C. *Now He Will Tell It to Everyone*
   1. Tell of the cross and its passion
   2. Tell of the cross and its power

II. Body
  A. *How Christians Are Identified with Christ (vv. 1–2)*
   1. The Christian is identified with Christ in His death, burial, and resurrection
    a. Galatians 2:20: I am crucified with Christ
    b. Romans 6:1–13: reckoned dead with Christ
   2. God the Father sees each Christian as crucified with Christ
   3. Now arm yourselves; make this your armor
    a. Speaks of a battle
    b. The Christian is in a battle with Satan
     (1) Consider the reality of Satan
     (2) 2 Corinthians 11:14 (angel of light); 1 Peter 5:8; 1 Thess. 3:5; 2 Cor. 11:3; 1 Thess.2:18; 2 Cor. 4:4; Eph. 2:2
   4. The new purpose in life
    a. The rest of his time in the flesh
    b. Nobody knows how long that will be
    c. Not to the lusts of men, just satisfying fleshly cravings
    d. But to the will of God
  B. *How Christians Are Identified with the World (vv. 3–6)*

1. "For the time past may suffice"; we've had enough of that
2. Now notice Peter reminds them how they used to live
   a. Like the Gentiles—the heathen and any unsaved
   b. Lasciviousness, lusts, excess of wine, revelings, drinking bouts
3. Some think it strange, some astonished that you don't run with them in the same flood of dissipation
4. They may talk about you
5. The purpose of it all is made clear at judgment

C. *How Christians Are Identified with Each Other (vv. 7–10)*
   1. Above all things have fervent charity (intense love) among yourselves
   2. What this love will do
      a. It will cover a multitude of sins. Whose sins? Saints' sins
      b. It will bring hospitality as a natural thing
   3. Blest be the tie that binds our hearts in Christian love

III. Conclusion
A. *Application and Call*
B. *To Saint and Sinner*

Back to Basics

1 Timothy 6:6–11

I. **Introduction**
   A. *Getting Back to the Basics in the Church*
      1. The importance of prayer
      2. The importance of loving one another
      3. The importance of caring for souls
      4. The importance of living each day in the light of His coming
   B. *Paul's Call for a Return to Basics in Daily Living*
      1. Success in the eyes of the world
      2. True success

II. **Body**
   A. *Godliness (v. 6)*
      1. Must begin with response to the gospel
         a. No way to achieve godliness apart from this
         b. Cannot read your way to godliness
         c. Cannot meditate your way to godliness
         d. Cannot work your way to godliness
         e. Cannot worship your way to godliness
         f. Cannot give your way to godliness
      2. But all these may be part of becoming godly after salvation
         a. The Bible: a route to godliness
         b. Prayer: a route to godliness
         c. Worship: a route to godliness
         d. Devotional life: a route to godliness
         e. No shortcuts
   B. *Contentment*
      1. Godliness and contentment—what a combination!
      2. The contradiction of those who claim one without the other
         a. No one can walk close to God while complaining
         b. No one can know true contentment apart from a walk with God
      3. Contentment comes from focusing on what we have

(Isa. 26:3)
4. Discontentment comes from focusing on what we do not have
C. *Understanding (vv. 9–10)*
1. The danger of being rich
2. Yet this is the goal of many people
3. The sorrows that accompany riches
a. The care of keeping such holdings
b. The danger to loved ones
c. Consider the lives of the "stars"
4. The love of money is the root of all evil
D. *Goals (v. 11)*
1. Righteousness: seek ye first the kingdom of God
2. Godliness: here it is again; near to the heart of God
3. Faith: the school of faith; the power of faith
4. Love: how we need it; the great need of churches
5. Patience: waiting for God to work out His will
6. Meekness: humility; Moses, a man God could use at last

III. Conclusion
A. *What Is God Doing in Your Life?*
B. *What Are Your Needs Today?*

Positions Changed

1 John 3:1–3

I. Introduction
  A. The Profit of the Study of the Book of 1 John
    1. Letter to Christians—for us
    2. To the worldly Christians (1 John 2:15–16)
    3. To the backbiter (1 John 3:14)
    4. To the doubtful (1 John 5:12–13)
  B. A Letter of Love and Judgment
    1. "Behold, what manner of love" (v. 1)
    2. "He that hath the Son hath life; and he that hath not
       the Son of God hath not life" (1 John 5:12)

II. Body
  A. The Position of the Christian with God the Father (v. 1)
    1. The unexplainable love of God
    2. How to become a child of God (John 1:12)
    3. Joint heirs with Christ (Rom. 8:16–17)
    4. Permanent (Rom. 8:38–39)
    5. Clothed in Christ's righteousness (2 Cor. 5:21)
    6. All spiritual blessings (Eph. 1:3)
  B. The Position of the Christian in the World (v. 1)
    1. A peculiar people (Titus 2:14)
    2. Persecuted people (John 15:20)
    3. Separate people (2 Cor. 6:17)
    4. The signs of life; a new creature
       a. The natural movements of growth
       b. The worldly crowd ought to drop you
  C. The Position of the Christian in the Future (v. 2)
    1. The age of fear and failing hearts
    2. Men's desire to know the future
    3. The surest thing in life (John 14; Acts 1; 1 Thess. 4)

III. Conclusion
  A. Position of the Unsaved Compared
    1. Stands unjust before God
    2. Popular with the world
    3. Future is death and hell

B. *Christ the Great Position Changer*
   1. Ten lepers (Luke 17:11–19)
   2. Man born blind (John 9)
   3. Demon-possessed man (Mark 5:1–20)
   4. Thief on a cross (Luke 23:39–43)
   5. Zacchaeus (Luke 19:1–10)
   6. You (John 6:37)

Needs at Christmas

Isaiah 6:1–8

I. **Introduction**
  A. *Isaiah, the Christmas Prophet*
    1. A virgin shall conceive (Isa. 7:14)
    2. His name shall be called Wonderful (Isa. 9:6–7)
    3. The coming of John the Baptist (Isa. 40:3–5)
    4. The coming death of Christ on the cross (Isa. 53)
    5. The millennial kingdom (Isa. 11; 35)
  B. *Before Isaiah Received These Insights, He Needed to Be Changed*
  C. *Isaiah Lived in a Desperate Time*
    1. Chapter 1: the wayward nation
    2. Chapter 5: the woes pronounced
    3. Meeting Isaiah's needs and ours

II. **Body**
  A. *A New Awareness of the Character of God (vv. 1–4)*
    1. Isaiah's vision answered the question: What is God like?
    2. Jesus also came to answer this question; came to reveal the Father
      a. God is all powerful: omnipotent; the sea; the healings
      b. God is all knowing: omniscient; "needed not that any should testify of man: for he knew what was in man" (John 2:25)
      c. God is eternal; Jesus: "before Abraham was, I am" (John 8:58)
    3. But Isaiah had to learn that God is holy
      a. Holy, Holy, Holy: the Trinity
      b. Moses: take the shoes off your feet, holy ground
      c. The incarnation is the greatest example of God's holiness
        (1) Luke 1:26–35: the holy one which was born
        (2) "O Holy Night"—and it was
        (3) Holy in His birth, in His life, and in His death

        d. Revelation: He is the Holy One
    4. And God has not changed: He is still holy
 B. *A New Awakening of Christian Conscience (vv. 5–6)*
    1. "Then said I, Woe is me!" Compare to preceding woes
    2. When Isaiah measured himself by God's standard—conviction
    3. Last days: consciences seared with a hot iron
        a. Old-fashioned honesty is hard to find
        b. Rubber-band convictions that stretch to the occasion
    4. Hear Isaiah's confession:
        a. "I am undone"
        b. "I am a man of unclean lips"
        c. "I dwell in the midst of a people of unclean lips"
    5. Note how specific he is
    6. Note also the clear message of forgiveness (v. 6)
    7. "Call his name JESUS, for he shall save his people from their sins" (Matt. 1:21)
 C. *A New Concern for the Souls of Men (v. 8)*
    1. The Lord's question: "Whom shall I send?"
    2. Isaiah's response: "Send me"
    3. People will pray almost anything else
    4. The message to the shepherds was a message of evangelism to all people
    5. Are you willing to go wherever He leads?

III. Conclusion
 A. *The Lord's Question Sounds This Christmas*
 B. *What Will Your Answer Be?*

No Room

Luke 2:7

I. Introduction
   A. A Familiar Text
      1. Often used for sermons at Christmas
      2. Yet we generally see but the surface
   B. What "No Room for Them in the Inn" Really Says

II. Body
   A. There Was No Room for Jesus in the Business of Bethlehem
      1. The great crowd there for paying taxes
      2. The place was just too busy for the Savior
      3. But there was greater business to be done
         a. Salvation is more important than sales
         b. Eternity is more important than earnings
         c. Peace with God is more important than profit
         d. The Master is more important than money
      4. What crowds Jesus out of your life?
   B. There Was No Room for Jesus in the Homes of Bethlehem
      1. The inn was also the innkeeper's home
      2. What busy places our homes have become
      3. Time for television, computers, and newspapers— but not for Jesus
      4. Time for community activities
      5. Time for entertainment
      6. No wonder the world is in trouble
   C. There Was No Room for Jesus in the Social Life of Bethlehem
      1. This world is not a friend of God
      2. Prepare to be in the minority
      3. Prepare also to have the only things that count live in you

III. Conclusion
   A. How Perfectly This Text Fits Our Lives Today
   B. Make Room in Your Heart for Christ

Gifts for the King

Matthew 2:1–11

I. **Introduction**
   A. *The Importance of the Wise Men*
   B. *The Mystery of These Men and Their Mission*
      1. More mystery than any other Christmas characters
      2. Do not know exactly where they came from
      3. Do not know exactly how many there were
      4. Do not know exactly when they arrived
      5. Do not know exactly when they saw the star
   C. *Some Things We Know About the Wise Men*
      1. We know they were wise men: *Magi*—Babylonian word
      2. We know they came from the east—Babylon (500 miles east)
      3. We know they came seeking a king
      4. We know they brought gifts to the Lord Jesus
   D. *Gifts for the King*

II. **Body**
   A. *The Royal King: Gold (v. 11)*
      1. Gold: the symbol for royalty, common everywhere
      2. Daniel 9:25: the Messiah prince
      3. Bible types concerning the gifts of gold
         a. Tabernacle and ark (Exod. 25:10–40)
         b. Heaven (Rev. 21:18–21)
      4. Need one with authority to forgive and justify
      5. One day to be King of Kings; every knee shall bow (Rom. 14:11)
   B. *The Priestly King: Frankincense (v. 11)*
      1. Frankincense commonly used for incense in temples
      2. Daniel 9:24: righteousness, priests, prayer
      3. Frankincense in the Bible and types
         a. A symbol of purity (Exod. 30:34–37)
         b. A king who is pure; even David fell
         c. The grain offering (Lev. 2:1–2, 15)
      4. God's purpose to bring righteousness in your life
      5. Sanctification

197

  C. *The Suffering King: Myrrh (v. 11)*
    1. Myrrh: commonly used at death as embalming spice
    2. Bitter: speaks of sorrow, suffering, and death
    3. To the wise men: Daniel 9:26—Messiah cut off
    4. Bible types
       a. Passover lamb and bitter herbs
       b. John 19:39: myrrh at Christ's death
    5. Must be crushed to be used

III. Conclusion
  A. *The Gospel in Gifts*
    1. Believe on the Lord: gold
    2. Jesus Christ: frankincense
    3. Be saved: myrrh
  B. *Our Royal, Pure, Priestly, Suffering Savior*

Unconditional Surrender to the Savior

Romans 6:11–13

I. **Introduction**
   A. *The Bible: Not Only Theological But Also Practical*
      1. To obey its message will not only change your position before God but also your practice before men
      2. Not only will change your record in heaven, but also your reputation before men
   B. *Shall We Continue in Sin That Grace May Abound? (Rom. 6:1)*
      1. Now saved and secure, so shall we live in sin?
      2. Oh! Let it never be thought!
   C. *Surrender to God*
      1. Knowing that you died with Christ
      2. That you are alive to God through Him

II. **Body**
   A. *Do Not Surrender to Self*
      1. Those things which only gratify the body
      2. Need only go back to Eden to remember that we are fallen
      3. Need only read a newspaper or watch the news to be convinced of it
      4. Bible evidence of the sinful capability of man's body
         a. Galatians 5: the works of the flesh
         b. Jesus makes the difference clear (John 3:6)
         c. Galatians 6:8: shall of the flesh reap corruption
         d. Ephesians 2:3; 2 Peter 2:18
      5. Biblical examples of men who had surrendered to the flesh
         a. Felix
         b. Rich young ruler
         c. Herod
         d. Demas
      6. He is also saying that you do not need to surrender to the flesh
   B. *Do Not Surrender to Satan*
      1. The assault from outside; remember Eden

      2. Those things which go against the gospel
      3. The flesh cries for indulgence and sin
      4. Satan calls for sin and indulgence with a design
      5. To steal, to kill, to destroy
      6. You do not need to surrender to Satan
  C. *Do Surrender to the Savior*
      1. Those things which glorify the Savior
      2. Yield your members to Him
        a. Voice: what good if not surrendered?
        b. Feet: what good if not surrendered?
        c. Talents: what good if not surrendered?
        d. Life: what good if not surrendered?
      3. You can surrender to Jesus

III. Conclusion

  A. *You Are the Servant to Whomever You Surrender*
      1. Servant of the flesh, servants of Satan
      2. Servants of the Savior
  B. *Overcomers*

The Walk of Faith

Matthew 14:22–33

I. Introduction
   A. *The Feeding of the Five Thousand*
1. The five loaves and two fishes
2. The next day, the "Bread of Life"

   B. *The Disciples Sent Away*
1. The Savior at prayer
2. The storm: the fourth watch, 3:00 a.m.

II. Body
   A. *The Beginning of the Walk of Faith (v. 28)*
1. Romans 5:1; Ephesians 2:8–9; Hebrews 11—without faith, impossible to please God
2. The desire to hear the voice of Jesus
3. The desire for something sure: Call me, bid me come
4. Jesus and His ready invitation: Come
5. Isaiah 1:16; Matthew 11:28; Revelation 22:17
6. Peter walked on the water

   B. *The Trial of the Walk of Faith (v. 30)*
1. The wind was boisterous
2. Peter's eyes in the wrong place, on the storm
3. Our storms: financial, health, temptation, persecution
4. 1 Peter 1:16

   C. *The Reward of Faith (vv. 30–32)*
1. The good, simple prayer of faith and need
2. "Immediately" He stretched forth His hand
3. The wind did not cease, yet Peter was lifted up on the waves
4. Same storm, same waves, but Peter is safe
5. The boat that could not sink

III. Conclusion
   A. *The Storm Ceased; the Effect on the Others*
1. The Great One, worthy of worship
2. The Son of God

B. *The Appeal and the Application*
    1. Many Christians looking at the waves
    2. Unsaved who need to start the walk of faith

Present with the Lord

Funeral Message   *2 Corinthians 5:8*

I. Introduction

    A. We Live in Temporary Temples
1. Our bodies finally wear out; our time on earth is limited
2. Seventy to eighty years, more or less

    B. What Happens to Christians at Death?
1. We are absent from the body and present with the Lord
2. Christians don't come to their own funerals
3. They are immediately in the presence of the Lord

    C. What Do Absent and Present Mean to _____

II. Body

    A. He/She Has Been Released from the Restrictions of the Body
1. Our bodies are wonders of creation (Gen. 2:7)
    a. Adam made from the dust of the ground
    b. Given life by the breath of God
    c. That breath of life passed on to generations
2. We are "fearfully and wonderfully made" (Ps. 139:14)
    a. Walking wonders from the Creator's hand
    b. Examples of divine diversity
    c. Able to accomplish many things
3. Still, life in the body has its limits (health, age)

    B. He/She Has Been Received into the Realms of Glory
1. The great instantaneous change: absent/present
    a. A negative—then a powerful positive
    b. Death itself is difficult; Jesus wept at a grave
2. Death here below means life up above
3. Present with the Lord means arriving in heaven (John 14:1–3)
    a. No doubts about where Jesus is
    b. No doubts about where _____ is
4. Descriptions of heaven fall short of reality

    C. *He/She Is Rejoicing with the Redeemed of the Ages*
       1. Think of meeting heroes of the ages
         a. Meeting those in God's hall of fame
         b. Names familiar to him/her through Bible study
       2. Meeting people he/she brought to Christ
       3. Best of all, he/she is with the Savior

III. Conclusion
    A. *What Does All This Have to Do with Today?*
    B. *Words of Comfort to Those Who Sorrow*
    C. *Are You Sure of Heaven? Settle the Question Today!*

Some Things to Remember at Dedication

Building Dedication   *2 Chronicles 7:14*

I. **Introduction**
   A. *Dedication Day in Jerusalem*
      1. Dedication of the temple built by Solomon
      2. David's long desire to build the temple
   B. *What a Day It Was!*
      1. The sacrifice that awaited on the altar was con-
         sumed by fire
      2. The glory of the Lord filled the house
      3. The king's tremendous offering: 22,000 oxen and
         120,000 sheep
      4. A day of praise and victory
   C. *This Is a Day of Praise and Victory for Us*
      1. A long-awaited day
      2. The people return (v. 10)
   D. *The Lord's Instruction at the End of the Dedication*

II. **Body**
   A. *Don't Forget Humility: "shall humble themselves"*
      1. God's call for humility at the end of that day of
         blessing
      2. We have a building here to be proud of and thank-
         ful for
      3. The Lord knew that our blessings can become our
         greatest danger
      4. The battle with pride
         a. Some proud of position, others of possessions
         b. Some proud of race, others of face
         c. Some proud of success, others of spirituality
      5. The Lord's description of a proud church (Rev.
         3:15–17)
   B. *Don't Forget to Pray: "and pray"*
      1. The ingredient without which nothing spiritual can
         be accomplished
      2. No miracle without prayer; no might without prayer
      3. The greatest untapped resource in the world
      4. The church that is not praying is playing
      5. When a church deserts its prayer meeting, you can

205

soon write "Ichabod" over the door because the glory has departed

6. This is also true in the spiritual life of the individual
7. The reason we do not pray
   a. We become self-sufficient, so we don't feel the need to pray
   b. We think we can make it, so we don't pray
   c. We forget the dangers on every side, so we don't pray

C. *Don't Forget to Seek His Face: "and seek my face"*
1. Sometimes when a church grows, its desire for a big name increases
2. Effort is made to associate well-known names with the church
3. Remember, "Jesus is the sweetest name I know"
4. Let's be concerned with the Lord Himself
   a. How can I tell you in words? You must experience it
   b. Personal business between you and the Lord
   c. I can tell you this: His face is the face of one crucified; His face is filled with compassion; His face bears the look of love; the face of Jesus

D. *Don't Forget to Turn from Sin: "and turn from their wicked ways"*
1. That day was a day of rejoicing, but days of repentance are needed
2. That statement, "Turn from their wicked ways"— what does it mean to you?
   a. Does it mean you turn from cursing and turn to Christ?
   b. Does it mean you turn from gossip and turn to God?
   c. From stealing, to the Savior?
   d. From booze, to the Bible? From Cheating? Adultery? Lying?
3. Whatever it is, the Lord will receive and forgive you!

III. **Conclusion**
   A. *This Is a Call to Revival. Will You Heed It?*
   B. *Application and Call*

The Wise Thing to Do This Year

New Year Sermon   *Romans 12:1–2*

I. **Introduction**
   A. *The Christian and the New Year*
      1. Not a message primarily of time but of eternity
      2. The eternal God cannot be measured in years
      3. Yet there are certain great truths that we face each new year
         a. The coming of Christ is one year nearer
         b. Death is one year nearer
         c. Opportunity for service is one year shorter
   B. *The Smart Thing to Do This Year: Your Reasonable Service*
      1. Due to the above, we are faced with both an anticipation and an urgency unknown to the world
      2. Psalm 90:12: apply our hearts to wisdom

II. **Body**
   A. *It Will Be Wise to Surrender to Christ (v. 1)*
      1. The formula for wise action in vv. 1–2
      2. Present your bodies a living sacrifice: real surrender
         a. *Present*: put at one's disposal
         b. The technical term for presenting the Levitical sacrifices
      3. This action is in "harmony with the highest reason"
         a. No scientific discovery will be higher than intelligent reason
         b. The world calls this fanaticism; Christ calls it wisdom
      4. The basis for such action
         a. The preceding verses and His power
         b. The preceding chapters and His passion
         c. The preceding testimony of the writer
         d. Summarized as "the mercies of God"
   B. *It Will Be Wise to Separate from the World (v. 2)*
      1. "And be not conformed to this world"
      2. The age of conformity
      3. The Prodigal Son in the pigpen (the smell, the company, the conversation—low!)

C. *It Will Be Wise to Shine for Christ (v. 2)*
   1. "Be ye transformed" means to take off one's mask
   2. Example is Matthew 17:2—the showing of Christ's glory
   3. Changing the outside to be consistent with the inside
   4. What ought to be shining through (Gal. 5:22–23)
   5. Shining and the renewing of the mind

III. Conclusion
  A. *The Need for a New Start in Many Lives Today*
  B. *Application and Call*

The Open Door

Revelation 3:8

I. Introduction
  A. *Understanding the Book of Revelation*
  1. Revelation 1:19: the outline
  2. The church age (Rev. 2–3)
  B. *The Church of Philadelphia*
  1. The fundamental church of the end time
  2. The open door

II. Body
  A. *The Open Door of Faith*
  1. The message of salvation by faith
    a. A message obscured by the dark ages
    b. The Bible was in the monasteries—men in misery
    c. Martin Luther . . . "the just shall live by faith" (Rom 1:17)
  2. The gospel: unchanged today; no new interpretations needed
  3. But faith is not just the door to salvation, it is also the way of life
  4. Adventures in faith are to be our daily experience
  5. The church is to live by faith and move by faith
    a. Was there a time when the church dared trust God more?
    b. A. W. Tozer: "God works as long as His people live daringly: He ceases when they no longer need His aid."
  6. Quotes from other men of faith
  B. *The Open Door of Prayer*
  1. The wonderful privilege of prayer
  2. Giants of prayer in the Old Testament
    a. The prayers of Moses
    b. The prayers of David
    c. The prayers of Elijah and Elisha
  3. The prayers of the New Testament
    a. The early church in prayer
    b. The prayer of Acts 4

   c. The prayers of the church for Peter in prison
   d. Paul and Silas in prison
  4. The prayers of great men of the past
   a. John Knox
   b. John Wesley
   c. George Müeller
  5. But God answers prayer today
   a. Do you remember a time of more power in prayer?
   b. Was there a time when prayer was your first resort?
   c. Has your prayer life deteriorated?
 C. The Open Door of Revival
  1. Perhaps Christianity's most misunderstood word
  2. Charles Finney: Revival is "the renewal of the first love of Christians, resulting in the awakening and conversion of sinners to God." Finney added, "A revival is nothing else than a beginning of obedience to God"
  3. Some consign revival only to days of the past. But God . . .
  4. You can be revived; sinners can be saved; there can be a new beginning

III. Conclusion
 A. Summary
 B. Application and Call

Christ's Suffering and Ours

1 Peter 3:18–22

I. **Introduction**
   A. *Difficult Portion of Scripture*
      1. Pages and pages on these problems
      2. William L. Pettingill: "There is mystery about these pages."
   B. *The Great Commentators Disagree*
      1. You find opinions by Augustine and Thomas Aquinas on one view
      2. You find Alford with another view; "The great majority of commentators"
      3. You find Calvin and Zwingli and Tertullian with yet another view
   C. *Often Good Not to Become Too Dogmatic on Portions on Which Great Men of God Do Not Agree*
      1. Sometimes we would like to just skip over these portions
      2. That would be easier, but someone is always asking questions

II. **Body**
   A. *The Controversial Part of This Portion of Scripture*
      1. What is meant by vv. 19–20?
         a. Did Christ descend into hell?
         b. Did He preach to the dead? (No)
         c. Did He give the dead another chance to be saved? (No)
         d. If so, was it only the dead who died before the flood? (No)
         e. Is it possible that all dead will have a second chance? (No)
      2. Some of the many answers
         a. Salvation offered to all dead before the cross
         b. The gospel announced but not offered—doesn't say He gave opportunity to be saved
         c. By His Spirit He preached through Noah in Noah's day

3. Author Roger Campbell on this controversial text
   a. It seems to stretch the text to make it mean that the preaching was through Noah
   b. It is inconsistent with Scripture to offer salvation to the dead (Heb. 9:27)
   c. Unthinkable that sinners in Noah's day should be privileged above all others—120 years (Gen. 6)
   d. It seems to me that the key to the passage is in the word *spirit*
     (1) Man is not a spirit—he has a spirit
     (2) I have never once found man, living or dead, who is called a spirit
     (3) Never once can I find man's spirit spoken of as imprisoned, even in hell
     (4) But angels are often called spirits (Ps. 104:4; Heb. 1:14)
     (5) Fallen angels are called evil spirits (Matt. 8:16; 10:1; Mark 3:11; 5:13–16; 6:7; 1 Tim. 4:1)
     (6) Some fallen angels are chained or imprisoned and awaiting judgment (2 Peter 2:4; Jude 6)
     (7) These are the angels involved in the awful sin before the flood
   e. Campbell's conclusion: Christ did go to preach to this group of fallen angels waiting in prison, informing them of His work upon the cross, thus increasing their condemnation
4. The key to the baptism verse is the word *figure*

B. *The Clear Part of the Portion*
  1. You could know all about Christ descending into hell, but if He does not come into your heart, you will be lost forever
  2. You could know all about the mysteries and not know the Master
  3. You could know all the secrets and not know salvation
  4. Let us look at the clear part of the portion
  5. Sin brings suffering
    a. It always has and always will

> > b. The garden of Eden, Cain, David, Saul, and others
> > c. Sin and death: the lot of the world because of sin
> > d. Christ died to bear the suffering of sin
> 6. Christ died for sinners
> > a. Not just for sins but for sinners
> > b. Not just to pay for sins but for my sins and your sins
> > c. The just for the unjust
> 7. Christ died for sinners that they might be saved
> > a. Have you been brought to God?
> > b. If not, you thwart the purposes of God for you

III. Conclusion
  A. *Respond to the Clear Call of God Today*
  B. *Application and Call*

The Sign of Noahic Conditions

Luke 17:26–27; Genesis 6

I. **Introduction**
   A. *Two Great Signs Considered Already*
      1. The sign of the nation of Israel
      2. The sign of the lineup of the nations
      3. Surely the time draws near
   B. *Jesus Instructed the Pharisees to Watch the Signs of the Times*
   C. *The Sign of the Days of Noah*

II. **Body**
   A. *The Noahic Age Was an Age of Material Abundance and Spiritual Poverty*
      1. "They did eat, they drank": speaks of a time of plenty
      2. The pre-flood age was one of lush vegetation
      3. No evidence of famine at any time before the flood
      4. In a natural way, vastly superior to the world today
      5. Fossils in the deserts show once inhabited by men
      6. Generally believed that even the Arctic and Antarctic were temperate
      7. Men's lot improves in a physical way around the world via war on poverty and aid to underdeveloped nations
      8. Spiritually, "a form of godliness, but denying the power thereof" (2 Tim. 3:5)
      9. Noah—preached for 120 years and only won his family
   B. *The Noahic Age Was an Age of Immorality (Luke 17:26–27; Gen. 6:2)*
      1. The most sacred earthly relationship is marriage
      2. Took wives—many wives, in and out of marriage
      3. The teaching of God's Word is designed to protect marriage: Thou shalt not commit adultery; 1 Corinthians 6:9–10; Sodom
      4. But now the scrapping of old and accepted standards

    5. The adopting of old and sinful ways: not a "new morality," just the adopting of the social habits of the days of Noah

    6. Let every filthy movie ad remind you that Jesus is coming

    7. Let every vile lowering of standards remind you that Jesus comes

C. *The Noahic Age Was an Age of Violence (Gen. 6:11–13)*

    1. The century of violence

    2. The century when the greatest minds in the world have been put to work to design ways of death

    3. The streets have become places for riots

    4. Revolution all over the world has become a way of life

    5. Can't be blamed on anything other than man's sinful nature

III. Conclusion

A. *Signs of His Coming Multiply*

B. *Let All These Things Shout, Jesus Is Coming!*

The Revelation of Jesus Christ

Revelation 1:1–8

I. Introduction
A. *Revelation: the Strange and Mysterious Book*
1. Shunned by some: they don't read because it is too deep
2. Doubted by others: seems too fantastic to be true
3. Twisted by many: source of many cults
B. *The Revelation of Revelation*
1. Revelation (Greek: *Apocalypse*): the unveiling
2. The aim to make it plain
3. Time covered; personalities involved; where and when

II. Body
A. *The Revelation of Jesus Christ to Those Whom He Has Loved and Washed from Their Sins in His Own Blood (v. 5)*
1. The future for the sinner is not bright
   a. He must stand before God naked in his sins
   b. No comforting word to those who are lost as to future
2. The future is only glorious to the blood-bought throng
   a. Recipients of Christ's love; He "that loved us"
   b. Cleansed from sin
3. Note scenes of men before the throne
   a. Revelation 6:15–17: before Christ in tribulation
   b. Revelation 20:11: before Christ in judgment
   c. Revelation 5:9: before Christ with sins gone
B. *The Revelation of Jesus Christ to Those Whom He Has Made a Kingdom of Priests unto God (v. 6)*
1. Kings: "kingdom" in original
2. A kingdom of priests
   a. The ideal (Exod. 19:6)
   b. Christ, our great high priest (Heb. 7:24)
   c. Christians: a royal priesthood (1 Peter 2:5, 9)
3. The priesthood and what it entails and means
   a. The priest is man's representative before God

  b. The tribe of Levi in Israel
  c. Men who talk with God for others (Eph. 2:18;
      1 Tim. 2:1–2)
  4. Development of this in the future kingdom
C. *The Revelation of Jesus Christ to Those with Whom He
    Will Come in Power and Great Glory (v. 7)*
  1. The two distinct phases of Christ's coming
      a. For the saints (John 14:3; Phil. 3:20; 1 Thess.
          4:15)
      b. With His saints (Zech. 14:4, 9; Col. 3:4; Jude
          14)
  2. He cometh with on a white horse (Rev. 19:11)
  3. Every eye shall see Him (Zech. 12:10)—contrast
      with first coming

III. **Conclusion**
  A. *Revelation Precious to Whom?*
    1. Whom He has cleansed
    2. With whom He communes
    3. With whom He will come
  B. *Christ Preparing His Own for the Future: the Blessing*
    1. Do you belong to Him?
    2. The risen Christ for this hour

The Satanic Trinity

I. **Introduction**
   A. *Satan's Desire to Be Like God (Isa. 14:12–14)*
      1. Satan's fall from his first and favored position
      2. The usurper—no wonder he institutes false religion
      3. Satan's desire for worship of man
   B. *Satan Ever Attempting to Thwart God's Plan of Redemption*
      1. Satan in the garden
      2. Satan and Israel; Satan and Christ
      3. The great attempt to ascend and war in heaven
   C. *The Satanic Trinity*

II. **Body**
   A. *The Dragon—Compares to the Father*
      1. Revelation 12:3–4, 13–14; 13:4
      2. The plan conceived: the most hideous of Satan's plans
      3. Just as God's plan of salvation is the greatest ever known
      4. God motivated for salvation's plan
         a. God's grace: "for by grace are ye saved" (Eph. 2:8)
         b. Love (Rom. 5: 8; John 3:16)
      5. Satan motivated for the final satanic plan
         a. Pride, jealousy toward God
         b. A liar and a murderer (John 8:44)
         c. The lawless one
   B. *The Beast (the Antichrist)—Compares to Christ*
      1. Comes on the scene when the earth is in great turmoil
      2. Symbolizes man in complete power: the Beast
         a. Look for everything to be more and more centralized
         b. All finances
         c. All education
         d. All labor and business
         e. All religion

3. Receives worship
4. Power was given to him (compare with Christ—all power)
5. Power from Satan (compare with Christ—power from God)
6. Forty two months (compare with Christ—an everlasting kingdom)
7. Satan incarnate is accepted (compare with Christ—was rejected)

C. *The False Prophet—Compares to the Holy Spirit*
   1. Speaks not of himself but of the Antichrist
   2. Religion and politics tied into one
   3. Calls down fire from heaven
   4. Does miracles; claims resurrection power
   5. The religious head

III. Conclusion
   A. *Accept the True Christ Today*
   B. *Listen to the Voice of the True Holy Spirit*

SCRIPTURE INDEX